HEART SPEAKS TO HEART

D0067728

TRADITIONS OF CHRISTIAN SPIRITUALITY SERIES

HEART SPEAKS TO HEART

The Salesian Tradition

WENDY M. WRIGHT

SERIES EDITOR:
Philip Sheldrake

ORBIS BOOKS
Maryknoll, New York 10545

Founded in 1970, Orbis Books endeavors to publish works that enlighten the mind, nourish the spirit, and challenge the conscience. The publishing arm of the Maryknoll Fathers & Brothers, Orbis seeks to explore the global dimensions of the Christian faith and mission, to invite dialogue with diverse cultures and religious traditions, and to serve the cause of reconciliation and peace. The books published reflect the views of their authors and do not represent the official position of the Society. To learn more about Maryknoll and Orbis Books, please visit our website at www.maryknoll.org.

First published in Great Britain in 2004 by
Darton, Longman and Todd Ltd
1 Spencer Court
140–142 Wandsworth High Street
London SW18 4JJ
Great Britain

First published in the USA in 2004 by
Orbis Books
P.O. Box 308
Maryknoll, New York 10545–0308
U.S.A.

Orbis ISBN 1–57075–506–X

Printed and bound in Great Britain.

Library of Congress Cataloging-in-Publication Data

Wright, Wendy M.
    Heart speaks to heart : the Salesian tradition / Wendy M. Wright
       p.   cm.—(Traditions of Christian spirituality series)
Includes bibliographical references.
    ISBN 1–57075–506–X
1. Salesians—Spiritual life. I. Title. II. Traditions of Christian spirituality.
    BX4045.W75 2003
    255'.79—dc21   2003010482

In memory
Joseph F. Powers, OSFS
(1935–2002)

Do not think about what will happen tomorrow, for the same eternal Father who takes care of you today will look out for you tomorrow and always. Either He will keep you from evil or He will give you invincible courage to endure it. Remain in peace.

St Francis de Sales

CONTENTS

PREFACE TO THE SERIES

Nowadays, in the Western world, there is a widespread hunger for spirituality in all its forms. This is not confined to traditional religious people, let alone to regular churchgoers. The desire for resources to sustain the spiritual quest has led many people to seek wisdom in unfamiliar places. Some have turned to cultures other than their own. The fascination with Native American or Aboriginal Australian spiritualities is a case in point. Other people have been attracted by the religions of India and Tibet or the Jewish Kabbalah and Sufi mysticism. One problem is that, in comparison to other religions, Christianity is not always associated in people's minds with 'spirituality'. The exceptions are a few figures from the past who have achieved almost cult status such as Hildegard of Bingen or Meister Eckhart. This is a great pity, for Christianity East and West over two thousand years has given birth to an immense range of spiritual wisdom. Many traditions continue to be active today. Others that were forgotten are being rediscovered and reinterpreted.

It is a long time since an extended series of introductions to Christian spiritual traditions has been available in English. Given the present climate, it is an opportune moment for a new series which will help more people to be aware of the great spiritual riches available within the Christian tradition.

The overall purpose of the series is to make selected spiritual traditions available to a contemporary readership. The books seek to provide accurate and balanced historical and thematic treatments of their subjects. The authors are also conscious of the need to make connections with contemporary experience and values without being artificial or reducing a tradition to one dimension. The authors are well versed in reliable scholarship about the traditions they describe. However, their intention is that the books should be fresh in style and accessible to the general reader.

One problem that such a series inevitably faces is the word 'spirituality'. For example, it is increasingly used beyond religious circles and does not necessarily imply a faith tradition. Again, it could mean substantially different things for a Christian and a Buddhist. Within Christianity itself, the word in its modern sense is relatively recent. The reality that it stands for differs subtly in the different contexts of time and place. Historically, 'spirituality' covers a breadth of human experience and a wide range of values and practices.

No single definition of 'spirituality' has been imposed on the authors in this series. Yet, despite the breadth of the series there is a sense of a common core in the writers themselves and in the traditions they describe. All Christian spiritual traditions have their source in three things. First, while drawing on ordinary experience and even religious insights from elsewhere, Christian spiritualities are rooted in the Scriptures and particularly in the Gospels. Second, spiritual traditions are not derived from abstract theory but from attempts to live out gospel values in a positive yet critical way within specific historical and cultural contexts. Third, the experiences and insights of individuals and groups are not isolated but are related to the wider Christian tradition of beliefs, practices and community life. From a Christian perspective, spirituality is not just concerned with prayer or even with narrowly religious activities. It concerns the whole of human life, viewed in terms of a conscious relationship with God, in Jesus Christ, through the indwelling of the Holy Spirit and within a community of believers.

The series as a whole includes traditions that probably would not have appeared twenty years ago. The authors themselves have been encouraged to challenge, where appropriate, inaccurate assumptions about their particular tradition. While conscious of their own biases, authors have none the less sought to correct the imbalances of the past. Previous understandings of what is mainstream or 'orthodox' sometimes need to be questioned. People or practices that became marginal demand to be re-examined. Studies of spirituality in the past frequently underestimated or ignored the role of women. Sometimes the treatments of spiritual traditions were culturally one-sided because they were written from an uncritical Western European or North Atlantic perspective.

However, any series is necessarily selective. It cannot hope to do full justice to the extraordinary variety of Christian spiritual traditions. The principles of selection are inevitably open to question. I hope that an appropriate balance has been maintained between a sense of the likely readership on the one hand and the dangers of narrowness on the other. In the end, choices had to be made and the result is inevitably weighted in favour of traditions that have achieved 'classic' status or which seem to capture the contemporary imagination. Within these limits, I trust that the series will offer a reasonably balanced account of what the Christian spiritual tradition has to offer.

As editor of the series I would like to thank all the authors who agreed to contribute and for the stimulating conversations and correspondence that sometimes resulted. I am especially grateful for the high quality of their work which made my task so much easier. Editing such a series is a complex undertaking. I have worked closely throughout with the editorial team of Darton, Longman and Todd and Robert Ellsberg of Orbis Books. I am immensely grateful to them for their friendly support and judicious advice. Without them this series would never have come together.

PHILIP SHELDRAKE
Sarum College, Salisbury

PREFACE AND ACKNOWLEDGEMENTS

This study of the Salesian spiritual tradition might more aptly be described as a prologue to the study of that tradition. In part this is the case because any brief survey of a tradition of any duration and depth is little more than an invitation for the reader to delve further into its richness. But this study is a prologue in another sense. Unlike its better-known and ancient counterparts such as the Benedictine, Franciscan, Dominican or Carmelite traditions, the Salesian tradition has not received the same breadth of critical scholarly attention as have its older analogues. Certainly there are fine critical sources now available for the tradition's sainted seventeenth-century founders, Francis de Sales and Jane de Chantal, and new studies, especially in French, are regularly appearing about the community of the Visitation that these two founded, as are studies of the late seventeenth-century Visitandine, Margaret Mary Alacoque. But beyond the seventeenth century the tradition is institutionally diffuse and extends into many corners of the Christian world through a variety of channels, including the writings of de Sales. Its nineteenth- and twentieth-century expressions, with the exception of that part of the tradition carried forward by the Salesians of Don Bosco (which is amply studied), are still yet to be mined by scholars. Records of Salesian spirituality from that later period circulate mainly in the form of pious tales or rest hidden in manuscript form in monastery archives or provincial offices. Thus, this particular study is not only an invitation to readers to read further but an invitation to scholars to begin the necessary work of careful, critical research into the texts, persons, ideas and institutional life of this most beautiful of Christian spiritual traditions.

Like an early modern cartographer, I have drawn here what I trust is an accurate, if preliminary, map that can guide future explorers and settlers who will chart the terrain and fill in all the minute details that make from a map an actual living landscape. Because the tradition's history is so little known and so little studied, I have included more information in the notes than might be thought usual in an introductory book like this. I hope this will not deter the general reader and will serve as a helpful guide to those who wish to continue their study.

I have employed the convention of using the English version of names of well-known figures. Thus François de Sales, Jeanne de Chantal, Marguerite-Marie Alacoque and Giovanni Bosco appear here as they are known in the English-speaking world – as Francis, Jane, Margaret Mary and John or Don Bosco. I have retained the original language spellings of lesser-known figures.

It is always true that any book is aided by the work and advice of others. With this book that is especially true. Its creation would be inconceivable without the collaboration of a small but vibrant cohort of other Salesian colleagues. Over the course of the last decade we have met, somewhat irregularly and in different settings, to explore together our shared heritage. Thus this book reflects the original contributions of seminar members Joseph Chorpenning, OSFS, Alexander Pocetto, OSFS, Joseph Boenzi, SDB, Péronne-Marie Thibert, VHM, Mary Grace McCormack, VHM, Mary Paula McCarthy, VHM, Dan Wisniewski, OSFS, Michael McGrath, OSFS, Robert McGilvray, OSFS, James Cryan, OSFS, Ruth Cunnings, Dr Roberta Brown, Dr Nancy Bowden, Susanne Koch, Dr Hélène Bordes, the late William Marceau, CSB, Mada-anne Gell, VHM, Thomas Dailey, OSFS, Jean-Marie Lemaire, and Dr Terry McGoldrick. (A very special thank you to the first six mentioned seminar members for their careful reading and attentive correction of this manuscript.) The book also reflects the unparalleled influence of Mary Patricia Burns, VHM, and the help and inspiration of Jeanne Johnson, VHM, Michael Murray, OSFS, Susan Gardiner, Tom Helfrich, OSFS, John Kasper, OSFS, Philomena Tisinger, VHM, Mary de Sales McNabb, VHM, Mary Berchmans, VHM, Louis Fiorelli, OSFS, Don Heet, OSFS, Jim Greenfield, OSFS, Mary Virginia Schmidt, VHM, Mary Frances Reis, VHM, Karen Mohan, VHM, Mary Margaret McKenzie, VHM, Dr Tony Lo-Presti, the Oblate Sisters of St Francis de Sales of Childs Maryland, all the sisters of the Visitation communities especially those of St Paul, Minneapolis, Georgetown, Federal Way (now closed), St Louis and Annecy, the East and West coast American provinces of the Oblates of St Francis de Sales as well as Joanne Kinney, Audrey Agnello, and John Graden, OSFS at De Sales Resource Center. I am especially grateful to Brendan Walsh, Philip Sheldrake and the staff at Darton, Longman and Todd for their shepherding this book so sensitively and helpfully. Thanks.

This book owes its greatest and inestimable debt to the organiser of the Salesian seminars and founder of the De Sales Resource Center, the late Joseph F. Powers, OSFS. It was Joe who over the last twenty years was colleague, collaborator, scholarly mentor, inspiration and friend. Through his many efforts – with laity, his Oblate confrères, fellow priests, Visitandines and scholars – the entire Salesian family has begun to acknowledge its shared spiritual heritage. It is to his memory that this book is lovingly dedicated.

1. THE SALESIAN SPIRITUAL TRADITION

In his study of Pierre de Bérulle and the seventeenth-century French School of spirituality, William Thompson comments that 'We can . . . meaningfully speak of the French School when the master images and fundamental horizon of thought are shared in common, even allowing for and wanting original modulations of the master metaphor.'[1] This observation also applies nicely to the Salesian spiritual tradition, a school of spirituality that shares some temporal and family commonalities with the French School.[2] Unlike many more famous spiritual schools whose master metaphors are articulated through history by highly visible networks of religious institutions – the Franciscans, Dominicans, Benedictines and Carmelites, for example – the Salesian tradition is more institutionally diffuse and its parameters somewhat less clearly delineated. Yet there is a distinct Salesian spiritual family whose horizon of thought was charted at the dawn of the seventeenth century in the era of early modern Catholicism and whose broad vision continues to nurture Christian holiness to this day.

Francis de Sales (1567–1622), French-speaking Savoyard bishop, charismatic preacher, noted writer and spiritual guide, is the tradition's most immediately recognisable figure. It is Francis who is generally seen as the founder of the Salesian school of spirituality. Indeed, his unique vision of the Christian life and the metaphors he employed in spiritual guidance and in his popular writings, especially his *Introduction to the Devout Life*, have truly shaped the tradition. But the early Salesian tradition was also shaped by a French woman, Jane de Chantal (1572–1641), Francis' spiritual friend and co-founder of the Visitation of Holy Mary.[3] This unusual women's community was the fruit of their shared love of God and vision of a revitalised Christian society in which people from many different walks of life and circumstances could become devout followers of Christ and leaven the loaf of Church renewal. For nineteen years after Francis' death, Jane was the person who gave direction and institutional solidity to the Visitation. The tradition thus bears her particular stamp as well as his.

After the passing of the founding mother and father, Salesian spirituality was carried through two chief avenues: the writings and reputation of Francis de Sales and the Order of the Visitation. That Order quickly gained popularity inside and outside France, influencing and being influenced by the spiritual currents of Catholicism in the later seventeenth and eighteenth centuries. The Visitation Order especially became the seedbed for and promoter of the increasingly popular devotion to the Sacred Heart of Jesus. Visitandine Margaret Mary Alacoque (1647–1690) is closely associated with that devotion. The Sacred Heart eventually became the standard flown over Catholic monarchist and loyalist (and thus anti-revolutionary and anti-republican) forces during the French Revolution. It also became the standard flown over the entire Catholic world in its early twentieth-century resistance to 'modernism' – what it deemed the anti-clericalism, positivism and scientism of the modern world.

Although the Visitation Order was greatly and adversely affected by the French Revolution and the subsequent European political upheavals into the nineteenth century, the writings of Francis de Sales remained popular and circulated widely both in Catholic and Protestant circles. Mid nineteenth-century Salesian spirituality was given new impetus in diverse quarters. Indeed, the nineteenth century has been characterised as the 'Salesian Pentecost'.[4] Several new religious communities dedicated to revitalising a besieged church were founded under the patronage of de Sales or through the influence of the Visitation. In Savoy the Missionary Oblates of St

Francis de Sales of Annecy, sponsored by the Bishop of Annecy, Pierre Joseph Rey, and founded by Fr Pierre Mermier (1790–1862), and its cognate women's community, the Sisters of the Cross of Cavanod, founded in 1839 by Mother Echernier, emerged to conduct internal missions in a de-Christianised land. In the Piedmont, a young priest, John Bosco (1815–1888), established his active apostolic family under the Salesian aegis. This family came to include the Salesians of Don Bosco, the Daughters of Mary Help of Christians (which Don Bosco founded together with Mother Maria Mazzarello) and a Society of Co-operators. From Paris, Monseigneur de Ségur, an avid devotee of Francis de Sales, actively facilitated networks of Salesian groups in the capital and the provinces. As a consequence, Fr Henri Chaumont (1838–1896), along with Madame Carré de Malberg, created the Daughters of Francis de Sales for laywomen. In addition, Chaumont established a spiritual association for diocesan priests animated by Salesian principles. From these Parisian foundations issued the Salesian Missionaries of Mary Immaculate, a congregation in India, and the Fraternity of Francis de Sales, a laymen's pious society.

South of Paris, with the sponsorship of Ségur, Genevan Bishop Mermillod and Mother Marie de Sales Chappuis (1793–1875) of the Troyes Visitation, several other religious associations specifically guided by Salesian principles were born. Fr Louis Brisson, (1817–1908) with Léonie Aviat (1844–1914), established the Oblate Sisters of St Francis de Sales in 1871, and Brisson himself, with Mother Chappuis, founded a men's community, the Oblates of St Francis de Sales, four years later. These charismatic manifestations of the 'Salesian Pentecost' each carried forth the Salesian spirit in its unique way, expanding on or interpreting the tradition's master images and fundamental horizon of thought.

Overseas missions carried the Salesian spiritual tradition outside of Europe. The Visitation saw foundations in the British Isles, eastern and southern Europe, Latin America, and North America. The Missionaries of St Francis de Sales of Annecy became especially strong in India. The Visitation

Order was established in the New World and took on the work
of educating many of the young Catholic women in the new
American Republic. The Oblates and Oblate Sisters and the
Don Bosco Salesian family all achieved a global reach. In
the twenty-first century the Salesians of Don Bosco are the
third largest Catholic religious order in the world. Moreover,
the long-lived popularity (especially up until Vatican II) of
Francis de Sales' devotional writings for laypeople has continued the integration of Salesian spiritual principles into
Catholic and wider Christian circles worldwide.

At the centre of this spiritual tradition is a vision, first
articulated at the dawn of the seventeenth century, of a world
of conjoined human and divine hearts. So it is to the Savoyard
bishop, Francis de Sales, who gave Christianity that vision
and who gives his name to this distinct Christian spiritual
tradition, that one must turn. His thought, and to a lesser
extent the thought of other Salesian notables, is presented
here in its biographical context. It has been suggested that
all theology is biography. Certainly, any deeply assimilated
spiritual vision is not only acquired as theoretical knowledge
but is forged in the process of experience. Personal experience
is interpreted through the lens of a received religious heritage
and, in turn, that heritage is tested and tried through particular experience. In the process, a vast, rich religious
tradition such as Christianity ends up having many 'mansions'
in which its adherents might dwell, each fashioned from a wide
range of scripturally-based symbols interpreted and lovingly
extrapolated in differing circumstances. The biographical contexts of the Salesian luminaries – those who are seen as the
tradition's 'saints' – are thus essential to understanding the
spiritual visions that animated their lives.

Indeed, it is possible to see the 'saints' of any spiritual tradition, as did theologian Karl Rahner, as fearless pioneers who,
from the material of a new historical moment, forge new forms
of Christian living appropriate to their age. Those forms of
Christian life inspire later generations, who, in their turn,
elaborate the master metaphors posed by the pioneers. So it

is with the Salesian holy ones. While some may and some may not be recognised by the Roman Church as 'official' saints who are memorialised on the liturgical calendar, the Salesian lights remembered in this volume were, each in their way, daring travellers who followed the first Salesian pioneers and created new lifestyles, new practices, new communities and new insights drawn from a shared heritage that imagined the fullness of the human–divine reality as a world of hearts.

2. A WORLD OF HEARTS: FRANCIS DE SALES

> As soon as a person gives a little attention to divinity a sweet feeling within the heart is experienced which shows that God is God of the heart . . . This pleasure, this confidence that the human heart naturally has in God certainly comes from nowhere else than the congruity between God's goodness and our soul . . .[1] St Francis de Sales

It was said he spoke 'heart to heart'. The charismatic Bishop of Savoy did indeed capture the hearts of the congregations to whom he preached. He captured the hearts of others as well – the powerful at the French court, the spiritual élite in the salons of Paris, the numerous directees and correspondents who were within the circle of his pastoral care, the unlettered peasant woman whom he met on his underground journeys to re-Catholicise Calvinist Geneva, the deaf valet who served him for years. Francis de Sales' heart-to-heart style of communication struck his contemporaries as a particular quality of his personality.

> He received all comers with the same expression of quiet friendliness, and never turned anyone away, whatever his station in life; he always listened with unhurried calmness and for as long as people felt they needed to talk. People longed to have a taste of that great sweetness and serenity of heart which he invariably gave them and which helped people to open out to him with great confidence, especially when they wanted to talk about spiritual things.[2]

But the bishop's graciousness and approachability were not simply natural gifts. They were outward expressions of a quality of heart, a heart on which – as he said – was engraved the name of Jesus. *'Vive Jésus!'* ('Live Jesus!') was the motto he used. The motto was simple but underneath it lay an entire spiritual theology – a vision of a divine–human world of hearts.

EARLY YEARS

Francis de Sales was born in 1567, the first and longed-for child of a Savoyard nobleman, Monsieur de Boisy, and his young wife, Françoise de Sionnaz.[3] The child carried the name of the family estate on which he was born – the Château de Sales. He was his mother's delight, and he remained close to her throughout her life. As the firstborn hope for this aristocratic Catholic family, Francis was given a well-rounded gentleman's education in several schools in the vicinity of home. This was expected for a well-born son of Savoy.[4] At the age of about twelve he was sent to study at the Jesuit College of Clermont in Paris, a choice apparently his own because he had heard that students in other institutions were not as 'given to piety' as they were with the Society of Jesus. Crossing the boundaries of his natal duchy for the first time, Francis, always a sensitive child, became painfully aware of the devastation caused by years of religious warfare in France carried out in the wake of the seismic European cultural shifts known to later generations as the Renaissance and Reformation; ruined churches and shattered devotional statuary witnessed to the struggles between French Catholic loyalists and Huguenot Protestants.

The age of religious conflict into which the young de Sales was born was to give direction to his later life. But he was to be as much shaped by the vital reforming energy within Roman Catholicism as by the challenge of Protestantism without. In this era, aptly described as early modern Catholicism,[5] reform was in the air: reform of existing church institutions and the development of new structures to facilitate reform, the emergence of new reforming religious orders, the clarification of church teaching and the creation of processes by which clergy and lay education might be improved. Above all, this was an era of vibrant spiritual renewal. Everywhere laypersons, monastics and clerics were thirsting for the many new translations of classic devotional literature that were circulating as well as devouring newly written treatises. There was a vogue for mysticism and a taste for the visionary as well as a resurgence of interest in asceticism and the deeply committed Christian life realised in practice. At the college of Clermont the young Francis was intellectually and spiritually formed by the Christian humanist education offered by his Jesuit masters, that robust band shaped by the reforming fires of the age. The intellectually rigorous curriculum offered a broad classical education which culminated in philosophy and theology and was based on the assumption that all human capacities, including the arts and intellectual life, should be cultivated for the glory of God.[6] The solid Jesuit spiritual formation he received at Clermont encouraged the youthful Francis to be a 'contemplative in action', to seek God in all things and to spend himself generously in the service of Christ and the Church he believed was Christ's own.

In the course of his theological studies Francis was caught in the vortex of a spiritual crisis that was to have implications for the unique spiritual vision he would one day offer to the world. On reading the theories of Augustine and Thomas Aquinas on predestination, he was plunged into doubt about his own eternal salvation. The fierce deity who predestined some but not others to salvation was in contrast with the God of love Francis had come to adore. He was especially drawn to the God presented in the commentaries on the Song of Songs by his theology and Hebrew teacher, Benedictine Gilbert Génébrard. Through Génébrard, the young de Sales came to believe that the history of the world and of salvation was in fact the history of Love itself.[7] The imagery of the Song, its delightful depiction of the mutual dance of desire, was to saturate Francis' thought. How impossible it was then, for him to reconcile a God of predestination with this Bridegroom God he had come to embrace. The anguished struggle was resolved by making an heroic act of abandonment. 'I shall love You, Lord, in this life at least, if it is not granted me to love You in the eternal life . . . grant me, at least, not to be among those who will curse Your holy name.' As if in answer to his prayer, Francis was immediately cured of his despair.[8] This almost existential insight was the foundation upon which de Sales' profoundly 'optimistic' spirituality was to be constructed.[9] The idea of the infinitely loving providence of God coupled with a sense of freedom from fear and self-absorption pervaded all Francis' future thought. Thus he could write to a Madame de Veyssilieu in 1619 these characteristically Salesian thoughts:

> Do not think about what will happen tomorrow, for the same Eternal Father who takes care of you today will look out for you tomorrow and always. Either He will keep you from evil or He will give you invincible courage to endure it. Remain in peace. Rid your imagination of whatever troubles you.[10]

It was at his next place of study, the University of Padua, that the young student would undergo another crisis which would further inform his outlook. Padua was steeped in the air and art of the Italian Renaissance, and it was to its distinguished university that Francis' father sent him, intending that he study law. The dutiful son did study law but also embarked on a course of theological studies. And under the spiritual guidance of Jesuit Father Anthony Possevino, he nurtured a dream of entering the priesthood. In Padua the issue of predestination still troubled him. While the spiritual dimension of his earlier crisis was resolved, the intellectual component was not. Still wrestling with the question, Francis, with no small intellectual agitation, parted company with the interpreters of Augustine and Aquinas. He chose a theological position he felt was more worthy of God's grace and mercy, a position which rested upon biblical and evangelical texts and that affirmed that God wills to save all humankind, not only an elect few.[11] This view is the theoretical cornerstone of the spiritual vision of a world of hearts. Universal salvation might be what God willed but, Francis knew, it was up to each person to co-operate with the grace so fully offered. A life must be formed to respond to that loving grace. Thus, during his Padua years, Francis continued his own spiritual formation. He took to carrying with him and rereading each day the recently published ascetic manual *Spiritual Combat*, attributed to Theatine priest Lorenzo Scupoli, a work that aimed to perfect the soul through prayer, meditation and examination of conscience.

Further, to guide his life the earnest student wrote out his own set of *Spiritual Exercises* to aid him through each day. These rules of life would allow him to cultivate devotion in the often dissolute world of student life in which he was immersed. The rules consisted of an 'Exercise in Preparation of the Day' in which he was to imagine the day's upcoming events, anticipate any difficulties, resolve never to offend God in any way, and pray that the Lord's will be done in all things. 'Rules Governing the Day' included daily Mass, time for prayer ('the sacred sleep', in imitation of the beloved disciple John who rested on Jesus' breast), time for 'watchful repose,' and 'Rules for Conversations and Social Gatherings', which included limiting personal friendships to a few people of good character while maintaining cordial and respectful relations with all others.[12] These daily practices shaped the future bishop's interior life. They certainly anticipated the advice he would proffer to persons hungry for God in the *Introduction to the Devout Life*, published twenty years later. The influence of Ignatius Loyola's classic *Spiritual Exercises* is evident in this student handbook. Ignatius, founder of the Jesuits, had bequeathed to his Society a formidable retreat process centred on imaginative meditation on Scripture by means of which the retreatant is to realign his or her life with the life and mission of Christ. Francis himself practised the Ignatian *Exercises* several times. At the heart of the youthful Padua *Rules for Life* Francis placed the daily practice of the 'sacred sleep'.

As the body needs sleep to refresh and soothe its tired limbs, so does the soul need time to sleep and rest in the arms of its heavenly spouse to restore the strength and vigor of its spiritual powers that become exhausted and tired. Therefore, I will allot a certain time each day for this sacred sleep so that my soul, in imitation of the beloved disciple [John 13:23–24], will repose with complete confidence on the lovable breast, actually in the loving heart, of the Loving Savior.[13]

The exercise of sacred sleep consisted of a seven-point meditation intended to lead him to a profound experience of God's love and goodness. He began by calling to mind God's experienced graces, the beauty of virtue and a life of loving service, moved to considering the ugliness of sin and the misery of sinners contrasted with the wisdom revealed in the life, passion and death of Christ, and concluded with reflection on the beauty of divine justice, of the Virgin Mary, the saints, and the Trinity. All this culminated in Francis' resting on the breast of God.

Finally, I will rest in the love of the sole and unique goodness of God. I will taste, if I am able, this immense goodness, not in its effects but in itself. I will drink this water of life, not in the vessels or vials of creatures, but from its very source. I will savour how good this divine majesty is in itself, by itself, for itself.[14]

This contemplative practice of resting near the divine heart (one rooted deep in tradition) would seem to have sustained the Savoyard throughout his life and to have provided an experiential basis for his theological vision of the world of hearts.[15] That this practice was a continuous and fruitful one is evidenced by his dear friend Jane de Chantal's remembrance recalled two years after his death.

At Lyons (where I saw him for the last time) he said to me: 'Who could possibly disturb our peace? Even if everything went topsy turvy, I shouldn't let it worry me, for what does the whole wide world matter compared with peace of heart?' This steadfastness was the result, I think, of his watchful and vivid faith: for he saw everything, great or small, as coming from that divine providence in which he rested more peacefully than ever a beloved child lay on his mother's breast. He told us too, that our Lord had taught him this lesson from his youth . . .[16]

On completion of his education, Francis' father had planned for his son to embark on a distinguished law career, marry and inherit much of the family estate. But the graduate was set on belonging to God with an undivided heart. Eventually, with his mother's support, he won his father to his side. Francis promptly received Holy Orders and, as he was of prominent social status, soon was installed as provost or assistant to the Bishop of Geneva. Thus began his career as a man of the church. The early modern Catholic church to which the young provost had given his life was full of the vital energy of reform. Reform was taking place at all levels: in the episcopate and the priesthood; in traditional religious life through the foundation of innovative new religious communities like the Jesuits, the Barnabites, the Ursulines, the Congregation of the Oratory, the Discalced Carmelites and the Theatines; and through the revitalisation of the laity.[17] At the core of this reform was a lively spiritual renewal, a thirst for devotion fed by new translations and a newly composed literature of the spiritual life as well as zeal for direct charitable action to alleviate the ills of society.

MISSIONARY AND SPIRITUAL GUIDE

De Sales plunged into his new role with ardour, inspired by the legacy of the fabled Charles Borromeo of Milan, the very model of the Catholic reforming bishop. Francis' first expression of his zeal was to undertake a daring and dangerous mission into the Chablais territory. Although he was provost to the Bishop of Geneva, the bishop was not in residence in his see, for Geneva had become Calvinist territory a generation before; Catholic practice was forbidden there. At the behest of the Duke of Savoy, Francis aimed to reclaim the region of the Chablais for the Catholic cause. His weapons were not to be made of iron but the persuasive and charitable Word. In the course of the mission, Francis preached often in the face of opposition. In addition he encountered the threats of paid assassins and the misery of the Alpine cold. Future admirers loved to recall the night when, returning alone from his walking missionary visits to mountain villages in the Chablais, he was assailed by a pack of wolves. Climbing a nearby tree, he tied himself to a branch lest he fall off while he waited out the night and the patience of his would-be attackers. In his evangelical zeal the young priest even met to dialogue with noted Protestant theologian Theodore Beza. The young provost did not change Beza's mind but the mission met with some success. There were prominent conversions, which were celebrated and later remembered, and Catholic ritual practice was reintroduced into the region. More significantly, the Chablais mission confirmed the young prelate's intuition that persuasion – spoken from the heart in love – was preferable to battle, whether armed or in the form of invective intellectual debate.[18]

In the future the Savoyard's principal ministry was to be within the Roman Catholic fold, not in the mission field. After a four-year missionary stint, Francis was sent as a diplomatic emissary to France. There his horizons were expanded beyond provincial Savoy and he came into contact with the leading lights of the *milieu dévot*, leaders of the French spiritual Renaissance who met at the Parisian salon of Madame Barbe Acarie. Those frequenting the salon represented all the significant contemporary currents of Catholic spirituality. These included Pierre de Bérulle, remembered as the progenitor of the French School of spirituality that, with its Christocentric mysticism, came to dominate the Gallic church in the second half of the seventeenth century. Bérulle was also instrumental in establishing the French Oratory, a spiritual community dedicated to the renewal of the priesthood. With 'La Belle Acarie' and the support of the future Bishop de Sales, Bérulle introduced the Teresan Carmel into France. The French Carthusian Dom Beaucousin and the Englishman Benedict of Canfield brought to the salon their expertise in new methods of prayer and mortification derived from the Rheno-Flemish mystical tradition. Jesuit father Pierre Coton, confessor of the King and the French Dauphin, and Vincent de Paul, future founder of the Congregation of the Mission and the Daughters of Charity, also visited the Acarie circle. Francis moved easily in this company. In fact, Madame Acarie chose him as her confessor.

Francis himself would, for later generations, represent what has come to be known as the tradition of 'devout humanism'.[19] Literary historian Henri Brémond has described devout humanism as the belief that human beings possess 'relative sufficiency' to act on behalf of their own salvation. While wounded in the Fall, human nature retains a natural orientation to God as its end. Humans may exercise their essential goodness and co-operate with grace towards that end. Christian humanism also included a keen attention to Scripture and patristic writings as well as an appreciation of the wisdom of the classical world and of all the human arts because it is these arts that, through their beauty, draw humankind closer to the Divine Beauty.

The Savoyard managed to capture the hearts of not only the devout circle but also of all Paris. He preached publicly to acclamation, so charming King Henri IV that the monarch tried to lure Francis away from Savoy and annex him to the hierarchy of France. But Francis' deep attachment to his native soil and the town of Annecy where he resided – 'dear Nessy' he called it – as well as his sense of the necessity of episcopal diocesan residence allowed him to decline graciously.

BISHOP OF GENEVA: PREACHING AND TEACHING THE LOVE OF GOD

Upon his return to Savoy and the death of the previous bishop, the youthful de Sales was ordained to the episcopal office. In preparation he made a long retreat during which he dedicated himself to a life guided by the traditional apostolic ideal: poverty, almsgiving, prayer, confession and pastoral relations with his 'people', all sustained by daily prayer, spiritual reading and the Eucharist. These resolutions were not merely pious platitudes but heartfelt principles by which the new bishop conducted all his affairs. He did indeed live very simply, reducing the episcopal household and liberally giving alms. And he spent himself generously in service. He preached incessantly, catechised, reformed monasteries, made pastoral visits, and listened to innumerable confessions. Part of each day was spent attending to his voluminous correspondence, some of which concerned official business, but much of which concerned the spiritual guidance of the many people who sought his advice.

Bishop de Sales' fervent activity was motivated by the idealistic principles he had learned as a youth and as a student. He saw himself as about God's work in the radical renewal of the Church accomplished by raising up many devout people in all walks of life as leaven in the loaf of Christendom. Devotion, in the bishop's words '. . . is nothing else than a spiritual agility and liveliness by means of which charity realises its actions in us, or we do so by charity, promptly and lovingly'.[20]

Devotion, then, was simply living a life surrendered to love; prompted by the love of God, the devout person sought to love his or her neighbour. This description was not, of course, quite as obvious as it might seem since what the bishop defined was, simply, the Christian life. But he had a vivid sense of the particular way the Christian life might be lived most authentically. This was linked to the scriptural image found in Matthew 11.

Come to Me, all you who labour and are overburdened, and I will give you rest. Shoulder My yoke and learn from Me, for I am gentle and humble of heart, and you will find rest for your souls. (Matt. 11:28ff., NJB)

This Jesus of gentle and humble heart was the centrepiece of Francis de Sales' spiritual vision. Various strands of influence from his youth and early adulthood had combined to weave a spiritual tapestry depicting a 'world of hearts'. The pattern of this spiritual tapestry can, in fact, be visualised. God, in the Savoyard bishop's vision, is Love Itself. Although in essence beyond human description, God can metaphorically be said to be possessed of a Heart that is the source of all Love. God's Heart is life-giving, it is a womb, a fountain, a vital restless energy that breathes, pulses and beats. In its own economy the divine Heart is Trinitarian, and as such consists of the mutual and reciprocal love of Father and Son 'practiced in one sole aspiration sent forth reciprocally . . . this aspiration is but one aspiration or one Spirit sent forth by the two who breathe.'[21] The Godhead itself is thus imagined as relational and dynamic. In its fullness the Trinity, as it were, spills out of itself and overflows. Indeed, creation itself is the result of the intrinsic dynamic of Love that spills out, that gives of itself in abundance. In addition, the divine Heart imminent in creation acts relationally and dynamically. As Love gives, it also receives and is intent on drawing to itself all that it has created. Thus the Heart of God can be said to love human hearts and to long for union.

Human beings, according to the scriptural witness, are made in the image and likeness of God. For Salesian spirituality, this divine identity is most clearly realised in the human heart. (It is important to note that for Francis de Sales 'heart' does not connote merely sentiment, affection, or emotion. Instead it retains its biblical meaning as the core or centre of the person. Thus 'heart' involves intellect and reason as well as affection and will.) The human heart, created to know and love God is, like its divine counterpart, dynamic and relational.

It too breathes and beats. Through inspiration it draws in love. By aspiration it pours itself out towards its neighbour and its ultimate source. The human heart, it might be said, is made to beat in rhythm with the heart of God. Francis called the two motions of the loving heart, the 'love of complacence' (a receptive love) and the 'love of benevolence' (an active love).

God's eternal Heart and the created heart of humankind thus are designed for union. 'May God live in my heart for that is what it is made for', Francis was quoted as saying.[22] But clearly human hearts are 'arrhythmic'; they breathe and beat to a rhythm of their own. They are not at one with the heart of God. They are wounded or tarnished through original sin. What is needed is some intermediary heart that can bridge the human and divine realms, one heart that is both model and mediator that can transform human hearts and allow them to become what they were created to be. That heart is the crucified heart of Christ, the one who invites all to come and learn from Him for He is gentle and lowly of heart.

The Jesus of gentleness and humility is not a sentimental figure. In the Salesian world of hearts these qualities belong to God's own kingdom. If one looks carefully, one sees that the passage in Matthew 11 that issues its invitation is located in a scriptural discourse on the mystery of the kingdom of God. That mystery of the kingdom of God the Father, the passage continues, is revealed through the Son. 'Come to Me,' he declares, 'and learn from Me for I am gentle and humble of heart'. God's-kingdom-realised is thus seen in this gentle, humble heart that confounds and overturns the values of the accepted order. It is not power over others, self-assertion or wealth that characterise God's reign, but love of God and neighbour exercised through all the intimate, relational virtues like gentleness and humility. Salesian discipleship is thus first and foremost about an exchange of hearts. It is about the practice of 'living Jesus' through the cultivation of the little relational virtues. Discipleship is the lifelong opening of the heart to be transformed by and inhabited by Jesus' own gentle heart. In his *Introduction to the Devout Life* de Sales represented the divine imperative to his spiritual charges.

> 'Be converted to me with your whole heart,' God said. 'My son, give me your heart.' Since the heart is the source of our actions, as the heart is so are they. When the divine spouse invites the soul, he says, 'Put me as a seal on your heart, as a seal on your arm.' Yes, for whoever has Jesus Christ in his heart will soon have him in all his outward ways.
>
> For this reason . . . I have wished above all to engrave and inscribe on your heart this holy and sacred motto, 'Live Jesus!' . . . With St Paul, you can say these holy words. 'It is no longer I that live but Christ lives in me.' In short, whoever wins a person's heart has won the whole person.[23]

TEACHING THE LOVE OF OTHERS

Profound transformation of the human heart does not, however, take place solely between the individual and God. Human hearts beat not only in rhythm with the divine heartbeat but also with each other as well. Hearts that are claimed by the gentle Heart of Jesus inspire and draw other hearts to them, beating and breathing with the force of love. All forms of human communion and communication are therefore essential in the Salesian world of hearts. All are avenues through which love may flow. Created by and for love, women and men realise their true identity as they allow all their interactions to be gently guided by and attentive to the ultimate source of love. Preaching, writing, teaching, and guidance of any kind is imagined as 'winning hearts' by and for the gentle heart of Christ. In a remarkable letter of 1604, which is in fact a small treatise, Francis, the much sought-after preacher, advised Archbishop André Frémyot, Jane de Chantal's brother, on the art of preaching in such a way as to win hearts.

Preaching must be spontaneous, dignified, courageous,

natural, sturdy, devout, serious and a little slow . . . In a word . . . to speak with affection and devotion, with simplicity and candor, and with confidence, to be convinced of the doctrine we teach and of what we persuade. The supreme art is to have no art. Our words must be set aflame not by shouts and unrestrained gestures, but by inward affection. They must issue from our heart rather than from our mouth. We must speak well, but heart speaks to heart, and the tongue speaks only to men's ears.[24]

The ideal Salesian relationship is therefore a union of hearts forged out of a mutual desire for the fullness of love discovered in God who is Love Itself. All loves flow from the divine source: celibate love, married love, the love of God and the love of friends are all intertwined. Throughout his life Francis himself cultivated life-giving, loving relationships, especially spiritual friendships. Most notable is his nineteen-year friendship with Jane Frances Frémyot, Baroness de Chantal. It was with Jane that he founded the Visitation of Holy Mary, the women's community that was to be the ideal realisation of the Salesian world of hearts. Over the years these two friends in Christ communicated 'heart to heart', growing closer to their divine Beloved as they grew closer together. Of the strength of the bond of love that bound them Francis wrote:

I have never intended for there to be any connection between us that carries any obligation except that of love and true Christian friendship, whose binding force Saint Paul calls 'the bond of perfection'. And truly it is just that, for it is indissoluble and will not slacken. All other bonds are temporary, even that of vows of obedience which are broken by death and other occurrences. But the bond of love grows in time and takes on new power by enduring. It is exempt from the severance of death whose scythe cuts down everything except love: 'Love is as strong as death and more powerful than hell,' Solomon says . . . This is our bond, these are our chains which, the more they

restrain and press upon us, the more they give us ease
and liberty. Their power is only sweetness, their force only
gentleness, nothing is so pliable, nothing so solid as they
are. Therefore, consider me intimately linked with you
and do not be anxious to understand more about it except
that this bond is not contrary to any other bond, whether
it be of a vow or of marriage.[25]

The Savoyard's gift for friendship is also seen in his lifelong
friendship with Antoine Favre, president of the Senate of
Savoy, with whom Francis shared a homeland, a love of devotion, and a vision of a Christian humanist society. Together
the two friends founded the short-lived Florimontane Academy
– a centre for discussion and learning which concerned itself
with subjects as diverse as politics, rhetoric, cosmography,
geometry, languages, theology and philosophy. The men
remained close to the end, Favre being de Sales' right hand
man, his practical advisor, his counsellor, and his encouragement. In an almost daily communication, these two
remarkable friends gave themselves to each other within the
balance and boundaries of their duties to God, their families
and others.[26]

Spiritual friendship was vital for Francis himself and it
plays a crucial part in the Salesian world of hearts. For friendship is understood as a particular form of love, a mutual and
equal communication that, when rooted in a shared love of
God, becomes a spiritual path in itself. Heart to heart, friends
expand each other's capacity for love and encourage and challenge one another to move deeper into the divine embrace.
Monseigneur de Sales especially advised that persons 'in the
world' – lay people not dwelling in intentional spiritual community but raising families and doing the business of society
– find support in spiritual friends.

Along with supportive friends, lay people were encouraged
to seek out spiritual guides to help them live devoutly in the
midst of the busyness of family and work. De Sales himself
served as such a guide for many. He maintained a lively

correspondence with those who sought his advice on all sorts of matters from marriage, to prayer, the practice of virtue, and 'dangerous pastimes' like dancing. Into his personal correspondence he often slipped short generic reflections on the spiritual life that his correspondents could circulate among their own devout circles. Interestingly, most of the bishop's correspondents were women. He had a particular gift for their direction (a fact for which he was sometimes criticised: for why, it was questioned, would anyone waste so much time with such unimportant persons?). Among this group was a young matron, Louise de Charmoisy, wife of a Savoyard ambassador, to whom the bishop sent practical advice on living a devout life in the midst of the court. The letters of guidance to Madame de Charmoisy, along with others he had written to such friends as the Abbess Rose Bourgeois and her sister Madame Brûlart, were the basis for his first and most famous book, the *Introduction to the Devout Life*.

Francis taught Louise, Rose, and their friends that devotion was every human being's true vocation and could be lived in any profession or any circumstance. He was not the first in the Roman Catholic world to make such an assertion but he was certainly the one who popularised the notion and the one whose spiritual manual, the *Introduction*, was to become the classic guide for generations of lay faithful, Catholic and Protestant alike. The seventeenth-century Salesian call to a devout life would prefigure and lay the groundwork for the 'universal call to holiness' proclaimed in the seminal Catholic documents of the Second Vatican Council in the twentieth century.[27]

PASTORAL WORK

This spiritual tapestry, the dynamic, relational world of intertwined hearts, was the backdrop against which all of Bishop de Sales' actions were played out. Among the urgent pastoral tasks that confronted him were negotiations in the Chablais region to establish a viable Catholic presence through continued religious dialogue and the reform and adequate training of his own diocesan clergy. These tasks he approached with characteristic gentleness, relying upon persuasion and charity as methods of reform. He wished his priests to carry out their responsibilities with a like spirit and advised them,

> Have great cleanness and purity of conscience ... Have an ardent desire for the salvation of souls ... Have the prudence of a physician ... Above all, be charitable and discreet ... When you encounter some persons who, because of their serious sins ... are excessively over- whelmed and troubled in their conscience, you must lift up their spirit and console them by every possible means, assuring them of the great mercy of God, who is infinitely greater in pardoning them than are all the sins in the world in damning them, and you must promise to assist them in all that they will need from you for the salvation of their soul![28]

The many concerns that filled the bishop's days were all undertaken with this same spirit to which he invited his priests. Over the years he embarked on numerous exhausting pastoral visitations to the far regions of his diocese. While he took care of temporal administration, lawsuits and reconcili- ations, he preached incessantly heart to heart, concerning himself as much with humble, devout parishioners as with civic and church leaders. In fact, what was to become his most ambitious book, his masterwork *The Treatise on the Love of God*, seems to have been originally inspired by Francis' acquaintance with a simple village woman he met in the tiny market town of Amancy. This widow, manager of a modest dry goods and drapery store was, in the bishop's eyes, a great lover of God: generous to the poor, gently attentive to all she knew, and faithful in prayer. It was possibly the countrywoman's witness that encouraged Francis to take up his pen and begin the long-term writing project that was to become his master- piece and which early on he tentatively titled the *Life of Holy Charity*.[29]

This intense focus on the quality of a single human heart in the midst of the complex, political activity of a pastoral visitation was characteristic of Francis de Sales. He never lost sight of the uniqueness of each heart even though the list of important, history-making activities in which he was involved is long. In his ministry he most often became the agent of reconciliation, an episcopal responsibility he believed was essential to the office. For example, he was consulted by the papacy in the 1606 theological debate between Jesuits and Dominicans known to history as the affair *De Auxiliis*. At issue was the relationship between divine grace and human free will, the same thorny problem that had helped rend Christendom apart into Protestant and Catholic camps. Francis' solution was not dogmatic but existential and rooted in his personal hard-won spiritual struggle: God wills that all humans should be saved but in such a way that human liberty to consent to or reject grace is safeguarded. To those who consent, the desire for repentance and the gifts of charity and perseverance will also be offered.

Beyond this and in addition to the sometimes overwhelming demands of diocesan administration and his continual public preaching, Bishop de Sales' skills of reconciliation were sought in diplomatic circles. He negotiated in a 1616 Spanish–Savoyard conflict and later became a part of the Savoyard embassy that would request the hand of Princess Christine of France, sister of Louis XIII, for Victor Amedée of Piedmont, the Crown Prince of Savoy. This latter assignment embroiled him in the treacherous currents of French court politics alongside such formidable persons as Marie de Medici and Cardinal Richelieu. Remarkably Francis, who had no interest in the ostentation or intrigues so characteristic of the courts of Europe, did serve as a reconciling presence. He exercised his influence through what a contemporary termed 'the alliance that was effected in him among mystical contemplative virtue, charity in all its candor, and finesse of human judgment in all its wisdom'.[30]

Francis was very attentive to such public and political concerns, but in all of it his focus was clearly upon the mystery of the human heart and its free response to the invitation of an infinitely merciful God. The hearts of the rich and powerful and the hearts of those forgotten to history, all of these were the bishop's chief concern. Devotion, as he had instructed 'Philothea', his term for any reader of the *Introduction*, was a matter of the heart, an interior transformation which prompted outward action. One could 'Live Jesus!' behind the counter of a provincial dry goods store or as a retainer or noble at the royal court.

Thus his collected letters, while they cover a multitude of topics and are addressed to hundreds of varied correspondents, always read as though flowing from the pen of an inspired spiritual guide. This is what drew people to him: the quality of his own heart, inscribed as it was with the gentle name of Jesus. His contemporaries were also drawn to his charismatic preaching, although the transcriptions of his sermons perhaps speak less convincingly to twenty-first-century readers than do his other works.[31] It is, however, his two great books that have earned Francis de Sales his most esteemed place in the annals of Christian spirituality. In the scraps of time he carved out in the midst of his busy, busy life, the Bishop of Geneva wrote of his profoundly relational spirituality – the vision of a world of hearts.

THE *TREATISE* AND THE TWO WILLS OF GOD

The *Introduction to the Devout Life*, which grew out of his experience as a spiritual guide, was a practical manual of spiritual formation for lay people. His other, more ambitious work, the *Treatise on the Love of God*, probed more deeply into his foundational vision. This 'simple and clear' description of the 'birth, growth, decline, activities, benefits and perfection of God's love'[32] is Bishop de Sales' great canticle which sings of the reciprocal passionate love between human and divine hearts.

At the centre of the *Treatise*, in Books VIII and IX, lies the bishop's distinctive teaching on living between the two wills of God.[33] This teaching represents one of the key means by which one 'Lives Jesus' and the exchange of hearts takes place. As union with God is the purpose of human life and is a desire that lies deep within the heart, that desire must be purposely directed towards its true end. It is the will that is crucial in this union. The human will must be aligned to God's own will. According to de Sales, the divine will is in its essence unknowable. But there are two principal expressions of God's will available to human comprehension. The first Francis termed 'the signified will of God', that is, God's will known in the commandments, counsels, religious tradition and through 'inspiration'. In other words, the signified will is discovered through the traditional practice of discernment. One turns to Scripture, Church teaching, the lives of the saints, traditional practices (such as the works of mercy), the evangelical counsels (poverty, chastity and obedience), or the cultivation of the virtues. One seeks the advice of wise teachers, the counsel of trustworthy, spiritual guides and then, with conscience as guide, one discerns what 'God signifies' in any given situation. The love that moves one to discover this signified will de Sales calls 'the love of conformity'. Union with God's will is thus in part expressed by cleaving to, or conforming to the signified will.

The second avenue through which the divine will is available to human experience Francis calls 'the will of God's good pleasure'. Principally known in difficulties, either as unforeseen events, intractable situations, or physical and spiritual suffering, this will asks of the one who loves simply 'submission'. Here, the interior asceticism of Salesian spirituality is most evident. Love of submission to this 'will of God's good pleasure' may take the form of loving resignation or, eventually, a holy indifference in all things. In this way, the human will continues to fuse itself in loving union with the divine will.

The great genius in Francis de Sales' teaching on the two wills is discovered precisely in the spiritual art of living in the delicate tension *between* them. 'Let us live courageously between the one will of God and the other,' Francis wrote.[34] In other words, active, lively engagement in all things is required. One seeks to love God fully, to choose rightly, to walk faithfully, to grow in virtue, to use all one's human capacity to discern and follow what can be known of God's call in one's life. Especially in significant decisions, such as the choice of vocation – to priesthood, religious life or marriage – God's signified will is vigorously sought. Yet one must be flexible and generous enough to respond to that other manifestation of divine will – 'God's good pleasure'. In all that is not complicity in sin, the one who loves is invited to embrace illness, thwarted plans, obstacles, even spiritual dryness and anguish itself. Thus one's own will gradually aligns itself with the mystery of divine life. The fruit of this alignment of wills is pure love, the love of God above all things and for the sake of God alone. This is the love for which the human heart was created and to which it is called by the divine lover. Such a heart rests near the Heart of God.[35]

LAST YEARS

Despite the many remarkable accomplishments that history has recorded for Bishop de Sales, many of the visionary projects close to Francis' heart were never accomplished. Thonon, capital of the Chablais, never became the 'Catholic Geneva' that he envisioned. He was never able to establish a Jesuit college in his diocese or a seminary or an Oratory for priests. Each of these last projected establishments would have given real long-range institutional momentum to the spiritual renewal he knew to be of such significance in the nurture of a world of transformed hearts.[36] The little congregation of the Visitation, while it did flourish, was eventually altered in its structure and flexibility under the influence of others.

Motivated by the vision of a world of hearts and the desire to live into the vision, Francis de Sales did not spare himself. In the service of the Visitation, his diocese, the many who came to him for advice, the wider Church, the court and his own family, he poured himself out. 'Ask for nothing, refuse nothing: I have already said it many times,' he replied to Mother de Blonay, superior of the Visitation in Lyons when she asked him for a word that the Visitation sisters might engrave on their hearts. True to his motto, despite painful kidney stones and exhaustion incurred from a consultation at a General Chapter of the Bernardines, the bishop had responded when the Duke of Savoy requested his presence on a diplomatic mission to Avignon late in the year 1622.

With some premonition that his health would not allow him to return, Francis set out on the long journey in the bitter cold of winter. En route, he conducted business. Arriving at Lyons, he attended the many requisite liturgical events and festivals, heard confessions, preached, counselled, and received visitors. He also met with Jane de Chantal, who was travelling, although in a different direction, and discussed the business of their Order. Characteristically, he chose to lodge in the gardener's cottage in the grounds of the Lyons Visitation rather than in the sumptuous quarters where the rest of the entourage stayed. On 27 December, the Feast of John the Beloved Disciple, he collapsed. He died the next day at the age of fifty-five. The sudden death of the much-loved pastor, bishop, and spiritual guide was keenly felt not only by the assembled nobility but also by his many absent friends, including Antoine Favre and Jane de Chantal, as well as by the wider populace of the Savoy and France whom he had loved so much and to whom he had ministered heart to heart.

3. *LA SAINTE SOURCE*: JANE DE CHANTAL AND THE VISITATION OF HOLY MARY

> Since our Lord, in his goodness, has gathered our hearts into one, allow me, my dearest sisters, to greet you all, as a community and individually, for this same Lord will not allow me to greet you in any other way. But what a greeting it is! . . . LIVE JESUS! in our memory, in our will and in our actions! . . . Have a spirit of gentle cordiality toward one another . . . strive for that loving union of hearts . . .[1]
>
> St Jane de Chantal

She was a thirty-three year old widow when she first met the Bishop of Geneva.[2] Four years earlier her adored husband Christophe du Rabutin, Baron de Chantal, had been killed in a hunting accident, leaving the distraught baroness with four young children and a restless heart that sought solace in God. Jane Frances Frémyot, Baroness de Chantal, had come to the Lenten sermons in Dijon, the city of her birth, at the invitation of her father Bénigne Frémyot, a magistrate in the local parliament. For some time following her husband's death, she and her children had been living in difficult circumstances on the country estate of her father-in-law with his servant-mistress and their illegitimate offspring. Relatives had been pressing her to marry again, but Jane found a new desire emerging in her heart. As she had loved her husband passionately, she now found herself longing to give her life passionately to God. How that was to happen she had no inkling, but the prompting was there. Meanwhile, she had turned her attention to the education of her children (and her father-in-law's illegitimate children) as well as to the needs of the poor in the neighbourhood of the estate. The Lenten trip to Dijon was a welcome respite. The popular sermon series was to be preached by the charismatic bishop from Savoy. When Francis de Sales stepped out into the pulpit that March of 1604, an astonished Jane recognised him as the man who had recently appeared to her in a strange vision as, in her grief, she had been riding on her baronial estates.

SPIRITUAL FRIENDSHIP

Thus began one of the most fabled spiritual friendships in the annals of Christian history. The young widow, like many of her contemporaries, found in Francis de Sales an able director of souls. Over the course of several years, he introduced her to the essential practices of the spiritual life by helping her develop her own rule of life suited to her particular situation. She was hesitant at first, as anxious as a colt and constrained by bad spiritual advice formerly given to her by an inept guide; but gradually she grew more confident, free, and able to entrust herself to God's loving embrace. Her mentor introduced her to a set of moderate daily exercises that would gradually allow her to embrace the love that God offered her and to open her heart in return. While he advised certain practices, it was not slavish imitation that he aimed to encourage but a deep and generous responsiveness to the unique movement of the Spirit in her heart.

Madame,
This letter will assure you again and all the more that I shall very carefully keep the promise I made of writing you as often as I can. The greater the physical distance between us, the closer I feel is our interior bond. I shall never stop praying to God to perfect his work in you, that is, to further your excellent desire and plan to attain the

fullness of Christian life, a desire which you should cherish and nurture tenderly in your heart: consider it a work of the Holy Spirit and a spark of His divine flame . . . Every day presents opportunities for your desire to ripen . . . You may look upon this as one of the pillars of your tabernacle.

The other pillar is the love of your widowhood . . . The whole structure of your happiness rests on these two pillars. Once a month take a good look to see if one or the other of them has loosened; make use of some devout meditation similar to the one I am enclosing . . . Use it only if you really prefer it, for in everything and at all times I want you to have a holy liberty of spirit in the means you take to attain perfection. As long as the pillars of your tabernacle are in good condition and stable, it doesn't matter very much how you do this.

Be on your guard against scruples . . . keep yourself constantly in God's presence in the manner you already know. Avoid anxiety and worries, for nothing so impedes our progress toward perfection. Place your heart in our Lord's wounds gently, and not by force; have the utmost confidence that in His mercy and kindness He will not forsake you; yet, for all that, do not relax your hold on His holy cross.[3]

What her director was teaching her was to 'Live Jesus!', to make of her heart a vessel through which the divine life could enter the world.

Our souls must give birth, not outside themselves but inside themselves, to the sweetest, gentlest and most beautiful male child imaginable. It is Jesus whom we must bring to birth and produce in ourselves. You are pregnant with him, my dear sister, and blessed be God who is His Father.[4]

Her response was always ardent. From the beginning she longed to nurture the holy longings God had placed in her heart and she wanted nothing to come between herself and

her beloved. At a particularly difficult time, when family pressure to remarry was heightened, she heated a metal
instrument and engraved the name of Jesus on the flesh above
her heart, thus effectively rendering herself unable to wear
the low cut gowns that an eligible woman of her rank would
be obliged to wear in society. Her mentor admonished her –
and wished that the name of Jesus might be as ardently
engraved on her heart as it was on her flesh. But later reliable
memoirists would see the gesture as an act of spousal fidelity
of a bride of God, as well as a participation in the suffering of
the crucified One and a sign of Jane's mystical union with her
Beloved.[5]

Under Francis' tutelage the widowed baroness blossomed.
She learned to be patient in her waiting, content to love God
in whatever circumstances she found herself. As the years
passed, their relationship matured. More and more Jane
emerged as collaborator and friend to the bishop. They experienced their relationship as a 'bond of perfection', a mutual
spiritual path that drew them deeper into the love and service
of God.[6] Their bond of friendship is justly remembered not only
because of its beauty but also because it so clearly illustrates
the Salesian vision of a world of hearts. Very early on the
bishop sensed the power of their union: in each other they saw
mirrored their own deepest hopes and widest capacities. In
June 1604, just months after they had met, Francis could write

> ... from the first time that you consulted me about your
> interior life, God granted me a great love for your spirit.
> When you confessed to me in greater detail, a remarkable
> bond was forged in my soul that caused me to cherish your
> soul more and more. This made me write to you that God
> had given me to you, not thinking that it would ever
> be possible for the affection that I felt in my spirit to be
> increased – especially by praying to God for you. But now,
> my dear Daughter, a certain new quality has emerged
> which it seems I cannot describe, only its effect is a great
> interior sweetness that I have to wish for you a perfect

love of God and other spiritual blessings. No, I am not exaggerating the truth in the least, I speak before 'my heart's God' and yours. Each affection is different from others. The one I have for you has a certain quality which consoles me infinitely and, if all were known, is extremely profitable to me. Consider this an absolute truth and have no more doubts about it.[7]

The profound affection of their spiritual exchange, perhaps foreign to modern sensibilities, was facilitated by a long literary tradition of deeply-felt friendship. It also expressed their belief in the spiritual reality of hearts aflame with the love of God leading other hearts more deeply into the divine embrace. Their letters began to speak of 'our' heart, 'our' soul. This single union of persons sought the same good.

... it is true, my dear daughter, our unity is utterly consecrated to the highest unity and each day I sense more vividly the truth of our sincere connection which will not let me ever forget you even long, long after I have forgotten myself in order to better attach myself to the Cross.[8]

Jane was an ardent lover of God who continued to experience a call to give herself fully to her Beloved in an intentional way. Eventually, a vision of what that call might look like became clear between Jane and her director. The new form of life that after a number of years emerged from their shared discernment was spurred by Francis' exposure to Italian experimental religious communities and by the circumstances of Jane's own life. There were many women who, like the widow de Chantal, were profound lovers of God and felt a call to some sort of intentional religious life but who, because of advanced or tender age, widowed status, responsibility for children, frail health or physical disability, could not qualify as entrants to one of the austere reformed communities popular at the time. Women such as these needed a community with a flexible enclosure that would allow them, if need be, to attend to family business as well as to the needs of their immediate neighbours.

Moreover, they needed a moderate rule that emphasised interior rather than external discipline. Both friends rejoiced in their mutual commitment to institute a new women's religious congregation. Francis would write about their venture:

> You would not believe how much my heart was strengthened by our resolutions and by everything that contributed to their establishment. I feel an extraordinary sweetness about them as likewise I feel for the love I bear you. Because I love that love incomparably. It is strong, resilient, measureless and unreserved yet gentle, pliant, completely pure and tranquil. In short, if I am not deceived, it is completely in God.[9]

And Jane, on the eve of her profession to religious life in 1611, would write these glowing words about her new vocation.

> 'When will the happy day dawn?' The day when I shall again offer myself to my God, beyond recall? In his mercy he has given me an extraordinary and strong sense of this grace of belonging only to him; if it goes on as it is now, it will consume me altogether . . . Alas, the more I make up my mind to be really faithful to my divine Saviour, the more I realize that it is simply not possible to measure up to such great love. Oh how painful I find this barrier of feebleness! But why do I try to put it into words? This is just bringing God's gifts down to my own poor level, and I don't see how I can ever hope to express the love that calls me to live in perfect poverty, humble obedience and a most pure purity.[10]

A vision of this new life had opened to them after the sudden death of Francis' younger sister, who was for a period entrusted into Jane's care. Jane, while she had done all she could to prevent the death, was inconsolable. Some recompense had to be made. Soon, Jane's oldest daughter Marie Aymée was betrothed to Francis' brother; and because the bride was so young, it was clear that her mother should move to be closer to her. The young spouses – who were happily well suited – were to reside in Savoy. Thus Annecy, the bishop's residence, was chosen for the site of the new community's foundation. Jane's son Celse-Bénigne, her eldest, was a teenager of an age to go away to school: to this end he was sent to live with his uncle André Frémyot, the Archbishop of Bourges. Her two youngest daughters, Françoise and Charlotte, were to accompany their mother and live with the community, although Charlotte died suddenly of a fever before the plan was carried out. Françoise did accompany her mother to their new mountain home where she lived until maturity. When they came of age, Jane arranged marriages for Celse-Bénigne and Françoise. Madame de Chantal's arrangements for her children, over which she agonised, have not always been represented sympathetically by later ages. Suffice it to say that she never made them lightly but, with Francis as spiritual mentor, tried always to be a loving mother and to be faithful to the path she believed God had prepared for her.[11]

THE VISITATION OF HOLY MARY

What was this community of women to be? It was to be a concrete realisation of the world of hearts that the bishop, and now his friend Jane, saw as the authentic Christian life. It began in Annecy with three entrants – Madame de Chantal, her longtime family friend Charlotte de Bréchard, and Jacqueline Favre, daughter of Antoine Favre, Francis' dear companion. With them serving as 'out-sister' was Anne-Jacqueline Coste, a devout peasant woman Francis had met on his missionary journey to the Chablais, who had sheltered many an illegal Catholic in that Protestant land. The original plan for the community was simple. With Jane, Francis spent a considerable part of his years as bishop in the creation of this unique community. It gave concrete expression to several principles dear to both their hearts. When he was a student in Padua, Francis had been exposed to the innovative religious communities, both men's and women's, that had sprouted up

in the Italian peninsula. Among them, Frances of Rome's provided him with the example of a flexible diocesan congregation
for devout women who could give themselves both to prayer
and to service of their neighbours. As he later pursued his
episcopal duties, he became aware of a number of especially
devout women in his own diocese and in France who, for one
reason or another, had no particular place, no resting space as
it were, in the Church of the day where they might fully
respond to the call to love God with heart, mind and soul.
Since as the Salesian tradition envisioned it, the devout life
was first and foremost an interior matter, a matter of the
heart, it could be pursued in a multitude of forms. These
seemingly insignificant women might not be called to the fierce
asceticism of reformed Carmelite monasticism or to the
mission fields, but they might be called to the practice of
the little virtues in a community that would, through that
practice, become a microcosm of the larger world of human
and divine hearts. Living the dynamic tension between the
two wills of God, these simple women would enter into the true
liberty of the children of God, free to rest on the breast of their
Beloved in prayer and then, heart to heart, serve each other
and, as need arose, engage in modest service to the needy in
their immediate neighbourhood. Intended neither as a traditional contemplative, enclosed monastic foundation nor as
an active community with a specific apostolate, the realisation
of this women's congregation in his diocese, eventually to be
known as the Visitation of the Holy Mary,[12] was close to Bishop
Francis' and Madame de Chantal's hearts.[13]

Over a period of twelve years the two of them, with Jane de
Chantal as first novice, novice mistress and superior, steered
the little boat of the Visitation as it travelled from its first
modest moorings in the 'Gallery House' in Savoy into France
where it was transformed into a popular, flourishing vessel for
devout souls. The Visitation was to have a flexible structure –
they originally used the terms 'congregation', 'institute' or
'house' rather than order to describe it – since the absolute
enclosure, solemn vows, and papal approbation required for a

formal religious order would not pertain. Members took simple yearly renewable vows of poverty, chastity, and obedience that were not binding in canon law. While seclusion was emphasised to preserve an atmosphere of prayer, the walls which separated the women from 'the world' were supple. Widows might exit when extended family needs required. After the novitiate year, members might go out two by two to minister charitably to their neighbours as need required. In addition, married women in need of spiritual renewal might join the community for short periods for retreat. This flexible and innovative form of life was possible because it was a diocesan foundation, answerable to the local bishop rather than to Rome or a trans-national authority as were many of the more established women's orders. Daily life was ordered by the rhythm of the prayer of the Little Office of Our Lady, punctuated by periods of work (mainly household tasks), and time for personal reading and common recreation. This flexible and moderate rule was created to allow the house to become, in Jane's words, 'a tiny kingdom of charity'.

> Ah, my dear sisters, our beloved Visitation is a tiny kingdom of charity. If union and holy cherishing do not reign, it will soon be divided and consequently, laid waste, losing the luster which all the ingenuity of human effort could never regain . . . Let us therefore all pray that the Spirit of Love, uniter of hearts, grant us this close and living union with God by the total dependence of our will to His, and between us by a perfect cherishing and reciprocal union of heart and spirits, and in our little Institute by a mutual and exact conformity of life and affection, without talk of 'yours' and 'mine' ever occurring among us, and with our amiably serving each other to the greater Glory of God . . .[14]

It was the Virgin, dear to Jane's own heart since childhood, who was the patroness of the fledgling foundation.[15] And it was the biblical image of Mary's visit to her cousin Elizabeth (Luke 1:39–56) that summarised in iconic fashion the spirit of the new congregation.[16] The mystery of the Visitation for Jane and Francis summed up all the Christian mysteries, and as such it was first and foremost a mystery that expressed the dynamics of love. As divine love is ecstatic and communicative, pouring itself out into creation and drawing creation back to itself, the divine action in the world might be seen as a lover's visitation. Since love wants to be shared, it likes to visit.[17] Indeed, the mystery of the Incarnation, captured in the biblical scene of the Annunciation, was seen as God's 'kiss' to humanity, God's loving union with humankind through Mary, the spouse and lover. By this kiss creation is inspirited and the world transformed. Having been visited and prompted, Mary in her turn recapitulates this loving dynamic: she hastens to the hill country and the house of her cousin Elizabeth. There, these two pregnant women meet – one older, long barren and now expecting, the other young and ripe with Love's own longing for the world. Another visitation thus takes place. And as the mark of divine visitation is transformation, in the course of this most ordinary event of a cousins' reunion, the two women are transformed. They are transformed as the world is transformed by the action of God's love. In their heart to heart meeting these women are the image of both the individual and communal life inspired by the Spirit of love. 'The Visitation is . . . the path, the self-same sign of the Church throughout the ages in its movement toward the realisation of God's intent for the world.'[18]

The kingdom of God, the reign of divine love, is thus in Salesian spirituality aptly imaged as a visitation – a union of divine and human love, a love most vividly realised on earth as spiritual friendship. The reciprocity of the love of friends, that shared and mutually transforming relationship, is the model of the kingdom come. In a sermon given on 2 July 1618, the Feast of the Visitation, to the community that bore its name, Francis preached of ' . . . the Blessed Virgin . . . she not only possessed charity, but had received it in such plentitude that she was charity itself. She had conceived Him who, being all love, had transformed her into love itself . . .'[19]

According to the bishop, Mary's transformation into love was realised in the full flowering of the virtue of humility. Francis, as his meditative thought unfolded over the years, came to see the linkage between love and humility in a distinct way. Indeed, humility was to become one of the Visitation's most distinctive qualities. Jane and her daughters were to be true imitators of the Virgin. It was Mary's 'lowliness', her capacity to be a receptive vessel for God's initiative in the world, that allowed Love itself to be born. And just as her humility and love of God was fruitful, so the Virgin's humble service and love of her neighbours were also to bear fruit in her meeting with her cousin.

> Our Lady was not satisfied with having thus humbled herself before the Divine Majesty, for she well knew that humility and charity are not perfect until they are passed on to neighbor. From the love of God proceeds love of neighbor; and the great Apostle says: The greatness of your love for your brothers will be directly proportioned to the greatness of your love of God.[20]

Visitandines, like Mary, lived this mysterious synergy of a divine–human love that is at the same time receptive and active. And, like her, they did this in a hidden way. The life of love, the fully-lived life which is always a 'visitation' is radically transforming yet profoundly hidden. Like their biblical counterparts – two simple village women going about their women's work – the Visitation sisters guarded within themselves the cosmic secret of redemptive love. The mystery of the Visitation is thus revelatory of both the dynamism of the divine heart and of human hearts, and Salesian reflection on the mystery has implications for life beyond the women's community that bears its name. Spouses, friends, and any kind of human community: all are invited to a union of hearts that finds its deepest echo in the heart of God.

Francis' profound commentaries on the biblical mystery of the Visitation gave direction to the community that bore its name. Those commentaries developed over the years as he continued to plumb the dynamic implications of the world of hearts. For the bishop, the ever-widening action of trans-forming love did not cease with the salvific visitation of the angel to Mary and the visit of the two women in the hill country. God's kiss had inaugurated the redemptive activity of Christ in the world. Indeed, the 'Saviour in the womb' began His transforming work first in His mother and in His foster father Joseph, before His birth. Francis believed (as did some contemporaries) that Joseph had accompanied his espoused on her journey to her cousin Elizabeth. Joseph's heart was touched with affection for his putative son. The transforming visitation begun in the hill country thus radiated outward in ever expanding circles. From the Child, the transformation extended to Mary, Joseph, Elizabeth and her husband Zech-ariah. And soon, Love's dynamism could not be contained. The mutual, reciprocal love that was thus generated between and radiated out from the members of the Holy Family, upon which Francis frequently waxed eloquent, was in miniature an image of the Salesian world of hearts.[21]

THE LITTLE VIRTUES

The biblical mystery of the Visitation, whose symbolic meaning was lovingly articulated by the bishop and lived by the first superior, was the deep grammar out of which the fledgling congregation articulated its inner and outer life.[22] Its external practices were, as discussed, a moderate, flexible form of religious life that allowed for the twofold practice of love – for God and for one's neighbour. Prayer was the chief means by which love for God was nurtured. As for the second expression of love, the neighbours were, in part, those in need in the outlying community to whom the early sisters were to attend, but more specifically the community itself. Visitandines were to grow in love by 'Living Jesus' among themselves, by allowing their own hearts to be hollowed out by the practice of what Jane and Francis called the little virtues. Not everyone might be called to practise the heroic virtues, or asked to perform great works, but all could do little things with great love. Thus humility, patience, simplicity, kindness and gentleness would be the virtues that the Visitation sisters would cultivate.

Gentleness – *douceur* – is the virtue that is distinctive to Salesian spirituality, and the one, along with humility, that was plumbed deeply in the fledgling congregation.[23] Gentleness and humility were constitutive of the heart of Jesus who invited all to 'Come to Me and learn from Me, for I am gentle and humble of heart.' *Douceur* suggests being grace-filled or gracious both in external demeanour and in quality of heart. Gentleness was to be practised between and among members of the community. It was the characteristic way of the Visitation sister. In a letter written in 1624 to Charlotte de Bréchard, one of the founding mothers, Jane characterised the gentleness that should mark the Visitandine's life.

> In the name of God, my dear daughter, wait for the improvement of these good sisters with great patience, and bear with them gently. Treat their hearts affectionately, making them see their own faults without undue emotion or strong feelings or harshness, but so that through your help they will be encouraged to overcome them and still remain enamored of your material graciousness. This is the matchless way to win souls and it is characteristically ours.[24]

Indeed, the way in which Jane de Chantal went about guiding the women who joined the Visitation community with her unique style of spiritual guidance has been described as 'winning hearts' through gentle persuasion and encouragement.[25] Writing to another Visitandine in the community entrusted with guiding young souls, Jane wrote:

> I beg you, my dear Sister, govern your community with a great expansiveness of heart; give the sisters a holy liberty of spirit and banish from your mind and theirs a servile spirit of constraint. If a sister seems to lack confidence in you, don't, for that reason, show her the least coldness but

gain her trust through love and kindness ... the more solicitous, open and supportive you are with them, the more you will win their hearts. This is the best way of helping them advance toward the perfection of their vocation.[26]

Jane's own maternal capabilities were first formed in the care of her own children and honed by the spiritual practices she learned under the Savoyard bishop. They lent themselves well to guidance in the little virtues and the lived realisation of a world of hearts in the Visitation of Holy Mary. As first superior, she exhibited a mother's instinct for nurture and a sensitivity to the varied personalities that came to be in her charge. Hers was a distinctively Salesian method of guidance that Jane would instill in all the other women who would wear the mantle of spiritual motherhood in the new community. Much later she would write to a superior at the Visitation Monastery in Belley:

Well, God be eternally praised, my dearest daughter, for there you are now – mother! I beg His divine goodness to give you the spirit that is proper to spiritual mothers who, with a tender and cordial love, see to the advancement of souls, and who are never rushed, especially about temporal matters. The trust they place in the providence and love of their Spouse relieves them of all kinds of anxieties and makes them confident that He will see to all their needs, provided that they try to please Him by a perfect observance and by a trust in His goodness. That's the disposition I want for you, dearest; I can assure you that it will bring you many blessings.[27]

And to another she would write:

I exhort you, my dearest daughter, to encourage them [the novices] to advance in their love of their heavenly Spouse as much as you can, but do it with a spirit of gentleness, patience, and charity, which will in turn help you shoulder all their little weaknesses – their negligence, tardiness, and failings – without ever being surprised so that their perfect confidence in you might never be disturbed.[28]

THE MARTYRDOM OF LOVE

She had lived in the world as a daughter, wife, mother, and widow until she was thirty-eight. The remaining thirty-one years of Jane de Chantal's life were occupied as the foundress, first novice, first novice mistress, and first superior of a fledgling community. Hers was a full life. The historical record credits her with ably steering the barque of the Visitation as it increased in size and popularity. By the time Jane died in 1641, over eighty foundations were in existence. The Annecy monastery became known as the flagship of the entire fleet, the Sainte-Source (the Holy Source), to which the other monasteries looked for inspiration. The bonds between the autonomous houses were not primarily juridical but bonds of love and fidelity to the rules and customs of the Order. As the mission and vision of any religious community must be passed down through its constitutions and customs, this difficult task fell to the foundress. After her friend and mentor's death in 1622, Jane assumed primary responsibility for the Visitation's institutional continuity. It was she who saw to it that novice mistresses and superiors governed according to the Salesian spirit,[29] she who had to struggle to maintain the governmental structures that could ensure continuity of the charism, as when, years later, an apostolic visitor was almost imposed upon the community, a change she knew would alter the very core of their spirit.[30]

Even before Francis' death the Visitation had been altered from its original institutional form. Several years after the Annecy foundation, a group of women in Lyons, France sought to establish a Visitation house and, in the ensuing negotiations with the Cardinal-archbishop, the issue of enclosure had arisen. In Savoy under Bishop de Sales' jurisdiction the innovative community was possible. In France it met resistance. The outcome of the controversy changed what was a congregation into an Order observing formal vows. No longer would the sisters move in and out of the enclosure to visit the needy in the neighbourhood. In 1618 the Visitation was instituted as a canonically recognised contemplative order. Nonetheless, the distinctive interior spirit – the world of hearts – was retained, as was the moderate rule, and the practice of accepting widows, the handicapped, and the elderly. Jane accepted the transformation with characteristic willingness to embrace what she believed to be God's will: ' . . . suddenly we found ourselves differently inclined and with a great desire for cloister such as our Blessed Father has resolved . . .'[31]

Even though she was a capable administrator, such constant activity was not what the widow de Chantal had imagined for herself when she offered the remainder of her life to God. 'My spirit greatly loathes action,' she was to write late in life, 'and because I force myself to action as occasion demands, body and mind both feel crushed all the time'.[32] It was intimacy she sought, a heart to heart encounter with her divine Lover. This was her lifelong search. Despite the arduous administrative tasks that fell to her, Jane felt her true calling was a hidden, interior intimacy with God realised in prayer. As she matured in her practice, her prayer developed in a particular way, characteristically simple and contemplative. 'The presence of our spirit before His and His before ours . . . this is prayer,' she would write.[33] Simply holding oneself before God with all the loving attention with which one is able, whether or not one has elevated or profound thoughts or words – this, she believed, is all God asks. Jane's prayer, in fact the most distinctively Visitandine prayer, was the simplest and most humble: the loving desire of the heart and the willingness to suffer patiently in whatever God wills. This was the prayer she cultivated and taught her daughters in religion. Indeed, the foundress believed that this heart to heart intimacy was central to the institute's identity.

> . . . I have recognized that the almost universal attraction of the daughters of the Visitation is to a very simple

practice of the presence of God effected by a total abandonment of themselves to Holy Providence ... Several are
attracted this way from the beginning and it seems as
though God avails Himself of this one means to cause us
to achieve our end, and the perfect union of our soul with
Him. In short, I believe that this manner of prayer is
essential to our little Congregation, that it is a great gift
of God which requires infinite gratitude.[34]

This prayer of *simple rémise* or simple entrustment was both
filial and spousal. It mirrored the trust a child feels cradled in
a loving parent's arms as well as the surrender a lover experiences in the arms of a beloved. But the heart to heart intimacy
into which the Visitandines were drawn was not to remain
always a young love. As she matured in prayer, a Visitation
sister grew into a relationship with the Jesus who had died
on Calvary for love. The typical inner experience of Visitation
prayer was a mirror of that cruciform love.

Those who are led by this path are obligated to a great
purity of heart, humility, submission and total dependence
on God. They must greatly simplify their spirit in every
way, suppressing each reflection on the past, the present
and the future. And instead of looking to what they are
doing or will do, they must look to God, forgetting themselves as much as possible in all things in favor of this
continual remembrance, uniting their spirits with his
goodness, in everything that happens to them from
moment to moment. This should be done very simply.

What often happens to souls on this path is that they
are troubled by many distractions and that they continue
without any support from the senses. Our Lord withdraws
the feeling of his sweet presence from them as well as all
sorts of interior consolations and lights so that they
remain in total impotence and insensitivity, although
sometimes this is more true than others.

This somewhat surprises souls who are as yet inexperi-
enced. But they must remain firm and rest in God above

every thought and feeling, suffering, receiving and cherishing equally all the ways and works that God is pleased to perform in them, sacrificing themselves and unreservedly abandoning any of these works to the discretion of his love and very holy will, without seeing or wishing to see what they are doing or should do. But completely above their own sight and self-knowledge they must be joined in God in the supreme part of their spirit and be utterly lost in him. They will find, by this means, peace in the midst of war and rest in work. Simply put, we must remain in the state where God puts us: in pain, we must have patience, in suffering, we must endure.[35]

This generous, even austere, inner reality was Jane's as well as her spiritual daughters'. If one can speak of the human-divine relationship as a union of hearts and posit that to truly achieve intimacy, the human heart must become the heart of Jesus, then the pattern of that becoming is self-emptying. 'I no longer live but Christ lives in me': St Paul's words (Gal. 2:20) capture the trajectory of Madame de Chantal's life.

In a very real sense, Jane was Francis de Sales' most apt pupil. She dedicated the majority of her years to both ensuring that her mentor's memory was alive and that his vision of a world of hearts was realised in the Visitation Order. But Jane refracted the Salesian spirit in a personal and distinctive way.[36] Even before she met Bishop de Sales in Dijon in 1604, she had a keen thirst for radical unselfing. During the period of her mourning, the young widow received several spiritual insights. Once, God seemed to speak to her and say, 'As my Son Jesus was obedient, so I destine you for obedience.' A short time later, on her father-in-law's estate, she was shown 'that celestial love wanted to consume me in everything that was my own and that I would have many exterior and interior trials' yet 'to suffer for God seemed to me the taste of love on earth just as to possess God is its taste in heaven'.[37]

These early intimations would prove true. The mother superior would continue to experience what as a widow she had intuited. Throughout her life, Jane suffered from inner doubts against the faith, agitating 'temptations' against her own vocation and her decisions and great dryness in prayer. Although her contemporaries knew her as a woman of great composure with a reputation for sanctity, she silently suffered from the tremendous burden of administration and the embroilments into which the burgeoning Visitation was inevitably plunged. Her simple response to these inner and outer difficulties was to practise continual abandonment to what she perceived to be the will of God. Her unique practice of Salesian wisdom is seen clearly in her response to the disappointing last meeting she had with Francis in 1622. They were both on the road – he travelling as a chaplain to a royal entourage, she busy with the business of the Order – when they met in the parlour of the Visitation monastery in Lyons. Jane longed to speak of her inner life to her longtime confessor but there was no time. They spent what were to be their last hours together discussing community administration.

> She left Lyons with a blessing from the blessed prelate, whom she hoped to see again in Annecy, and she headed to our monastery in Grenoble. On the road, she was filled with a heartfelt sadness that our blessed father had not permitted her to speak of her inner life. But, not wishing to reflect on herself, nor to interpret what he had done, she made an act of abandonment to the divine will and, taking up her psalter in the carriage, she began to chant Psalm 26, 'The Lord is my light.' Several times she repeated the verse, 'If my father and mother desert me, the Lord will care for me still.' With this remedy, she was healed. This was her usual remedy for interior adversity: self-abandonment and several scripture verses.[38]

Similar was her practice when, a few short weeks later, she learned of her friend's sudden death.

> When M. Michel put the letter in my hand, my heart beat wildly. I surrendered myself to God and His will,

suspecting that it contained sad news. In the short space during which I was recollected, I understood the meaning of the phrase that was given to me in Grenoble: 'he is no more'. . . . I fell to my knees, adoring divine providence and embracing the holy will of God as best I could, and in the process, my incomparable affliction.[39]

Jane wept through the rest of the day into the evening.

At suppertime, she was unable to eat anything and retired early so the superior at Grenoble requested that a fine roast laced with sugar be sent to her room. The cook misunderstood and saturated the roast with salt rather than sugar, which our worthy mother nibbled at out of a love of submission. She then set the roast aside, unable to eat more. The superior, checking to see how she was, and discovering the briny roast, asked if Jane was feeling ill. She reported no sickness, adding that, 'she was in a state of finding nothing sweet but the will of God and nothing bitter but His terrible passion.[40]

In part because of background, temperament, and personal experience, Jane de Chantal brought her own emphasis to the divine–human love relationships, and thus to the Salesian world of hearts. Hers was a generous, unflinching teaching of 'pure love' – that continual abandonment, the love of obedience, and suffering are constituent components of living Jesus, and taking on His pierced and battered heart. Jane especially emphasised the constant practice of surrender to the will of God's good pleasure, that aspect of the divine will that is unbidden and about which Francis de Sales wrote so eloquently in the *Treatise on the Love of God*.

Expressive of her unique temper is a conversation she had in 1632 while at recreation with her Visitation sisters. The spontaneous talk was recorded by Françoise-Madeleine de Chaugy, one of her secretaries. Mother de Chaugy knew her superior well. A niece of Jane's own son-in-law, Françoise-Madeleine had been drawn into the Order through her contact

with her great aunt. Because of their long intimacy and Françoise-Madeleine's remarkable memory and literary gifts,
posterity knows something about the otherwise hidden experience of a very public yet very private woman. The occasion
was the feast of St Basil, one of the fathers of the early Church.

'My dear daughters, Saint Basil and most of the fathers
and pillars of the church were not martyred. Why do you
think this was so?' After each of us had tried to answer,
the Blessed Mother continued, 'For myself, I believe that
there is a martyrdom called the martyrdom of love in
which God preserves the lives of His servants so that they
might work for His glory. This makes them martyrs and
confessors at the same time. I know,' she added, 'that this
is the martyrdom to which the Daughters of the Visitation
are called and which God will allow them to suffer if
they are fortunate enough to wish for it.'

A sister asked how this martyrdom would be realized.
'Give your absolute consent to God and you experience it.
What happens,' she continued, 'is that divine love thrusts
its sword into the most intimate and secret parts of the
soul and separates us from our very selves. I know one
soul,' she added, 'whom love had severed in this way who
felt it more keenly than if a tyrant with his sword had
separated her body from her soul'. We knew very well that
she was speaking of herself. One sister wanted to know
how long this martyrdom might last 'From the moment,'
she responded, 'when we have given ourselves up unreservedly to God until the moment when we die. But this
is intended for generous hearts who, without holding
themselves back, are faithful to love. Hearts that are weak
and capable of only a little love and constancy are not
martyred by Our Lord. He is content to let them go on in
their little way so they won't fall by the wayside. God
never violates free will.' She was asked if this martyrdom
of love was ever equal to physical martyrdom. 'Don't
concern yourself with their equality,' she said, 'although I

think there is little difference between them because "love is strong as death," and martyrs of love suffer a thousand times more by staying alive to do God's will than if they had to give a thousand lives in witness of their faith, love and fidelity."[41]

This uncompromising sense of a life lived heart to heart with the crucified God of love is Jane's contribution to Salesian spirituality. It is, of course, present in Francis' own vision as well. It was he, in his *Treatise*, who described Mount Calvary as the Mount of Lovers. But Jane bequeathed to her daughters in the Visitation the lived example of the lover's destiny. Thus the twenty-first century editor of Jane's correspondence could write of the unique calling of the Visitation nun,

> At the Visitation, Love is the beginning, the means and the end of the spiritual life. In order to give herself over to Love's work, the Visitandine must let Love do what it will to strip her of anything else, any self-examination, any self-love. Love will purify her. She seeks only God's will. She lives in holy indifference to anything that is not love or the abandonment of love.[42]

LATER YEARS

In her last years Madame de Chantal facilitated the stunning success of the Visitation Order. It was a shining gem in the crown of the new vital religious communities that emerged in France in the seventeenth century.[43] At the same time her experience of personal loss was great. Of her four children, only one, Françoise, outlived her. The surviving correspondence between mother and daughter is telling. With the same gentle persistence she used with her nuns, Jane deftly guided this high-spirited daughter into her marriage with wealthy Monsieur de Toulonjon, then through the subsequent devastating losses of her children and husband. Jane's youngest, Charlotte, had died early, just before her mother entered the community. Marie-Aymée, who married Francis' brother Bernard, died in childbirth in her mother's arms at the age of nineteen, weakened by a succession of unsuccessful pregnancies. Jane's eldest, Celse-Bénigne, who during his lifetime had given his mother much grief (at one point he was exiled from the country for illegal duelling), married, had one daughter (the future Madame de Sevigné), then died in battle in 1627. Jane also outlived her first cherished companions in the Visitation. Out-sister Anne-Jacqueline Coste died in 1627. And in one year alone, 1637, her earliest and dearest friends Jacqueline Favre, Charlotte de Bréchard and Péronne-Marie de Châtel all passed away. Of course, she lost her friend Francis as well. Each of these losses cost her dearly. Only during the last months of her life, when she was able to lay down some of her administrative duties, did Jane experience release from the interior dryness and trials that had troubled her for years.

Jane succumbed to pneumonia in the Advent season of 1641. Having travelled to the monastery of Moulins on one of her frequent trips, she sensed the seriousness of the illness that came upon her. As doctors, her spiritual daughters and her friend the Countess of Montmorency tended her, she requested that, among other much-loved passages from Augustine and Jerome, the last chapter of the life of Francis de Sales, written by his nephew, be read aloud. She was much mourned, and her sisters in the numerouss Visitation communities would carry with them her memory and her particular embodiment of the experience of living heart to heart.

4. 'A GREAT LIGHT': DIFFUSION OF THE SALESIAN SPIRIT

> Our century has seen two great lights: one in Saint Charles Borromeo, the other in Blessed Francis de Sales, who now shine in the firmament of the church to honor God and His works and to enlighten all posterity.[1]
>
> Nicolas Caussin, SJ, *Treatise on Spiritual Conduct According to the Spirit of the Blessed Francis de Sales, Bishop and Prince of Geneva, 1637*

The deaths of the two founders of the Salesian tradition – Francis in 1622 and Jane in 1641 – closed an era. The vision of a world of hearts which they embodied and communicated to others so persuasively was now by necessity disseminated in new ways. The Order of the Visitation was the chief institutional channel through which the vision flowed and there were numerous Visitandines who, like the founders, embodied the vision for their generations. In addition, Francis' writings remained popular, were reprinted, translated, and spread abroad to create an astonishingly enduring and widespread literary legacy. Further, the reputations of the two founders were kept alive and enhanced through the publication of accounts of their lives and through the exemplary stories that continued to circulate and inspire generations of the faithful. An exhaustive account of the ubiquitous influence of Salesian spirituality on Catholic and Protestant thought and piety in the centuries following the founders' deaths is impossible, but a selective survey can give some sense of the diverse ways in

which the tradition continued, especially into the first decades
of the nineteenth century.

PORTRAITS OF THE FOUNDERS

It was not long after the charismatic bishop had been laid to
rest at the mother house of the Visitation in Annecy that his
contemporaries began to record their memories of him and to
claim for him a place in the communion of saints. One of the
first of these was his younger friend, Feuillant Dom Jean de
Saint-François, known to posterity as Jean Goulu, who published a life just two years after Francis' death. Goulu's
portrait was notable for its truth and simplicity as well as its
subtle depiction of the late bishop's distinctive spirit, an
unusual feature in biographies of the day. Much of the material
in the book was provided by Jane de Chantal herself. Goulu's
artful literary work became the basis of what later was to
become the standard early biography, the somewhat less felici-
tously written 1634 life by Francis' nephew Charles Auguste
de Sales, Provost of the Geneva chapter.[2]

In 1637, Jesuit spiritual writer and preacher Nicholas
Caussin published his laudatory *Treatise on Spiritual Conduct
According to the Spirit of the Blessed Francis de Sales, Bishop
and Prince of Geneva* which represented de Sales as a powerful
reforming bishop zealous to curb abuses in his diocese and as
a saint, possessed of all the beautiful and heroic virtues that
early modern Catholic sanctity implied. Caussin's Francis de
Sales was a model of spiritual equanimity and a prince of
Christian humanism who heroically co-operated with grace in
the perfection of love of God and one's neighbour. In part,
Caussin's heroic portrait was drawn to counter the notion that
Francis' gentleness and optimism were indulgent of human
weakness.[3] This muscular representation was typical of the
genre that influenced mid century readers.

Perhaps a bit less heroic, but certainly a very persuasive
and influential, spiritual picture of the Savoyard was drawn
by Jean-Pierre Camus, Bishop of Belley. Camus' credibility as

a portraitist was established by his long-term association with the elder bishop. In fact, Francis had consecrated the younger man to his episcopal appointment and over the course of years had served as his mentor and spiritual guide. *The Spirit of Francis de Sales*, like Caussin's book, was not a modern biography but a treatise arranged by spiritual topics: from perfect virtue, to desire, penance, spiritual desolation, and a bishop's care for his flock. Throughout, Camus quoted from or paraphrased Francis' own published words. But he was just as likely to recount an incident or anecdote or recall some statement he had heard the deceased make. Camus, a writer of novels as well as spiritual tracts, idolised de Sales and tried to capture his living example in as vivid a manner as possible. *The Spirit of Francis de Sales* caught on and the best known 1727 abridgment went through numerous editions not only in French but in German. There were also Italian and English translations, the last of these in 1952.[4] It is Camus' lively portrait that in great part conveyed the Salesian founder's spirit across the centuries.

Typical of Camus' account is the following.

> You know very well how Blessed Francis valued charity, but I will give you, nevertheless, some more of his teaching on this great subject.
>
> To a holy soul who had placed herself under his direction, he said: 'We must do all things from love, and nothing from constraint. We must love obedience rather than fear disobedience. I leave you the spirit of liberty: not such as excludes obedience, for that is the liberty of the flesh, but such as excludes constraint, scruples, and over-eagerness. However much you may love obedience and submission, I wish you to suspend for the moment the work in which obedience has engaged you whenever any just or charitable occasion for so doing occurs. This omission will be a species of obedience. Fill up its measure by charity.'
>
> From this spirit of holy and Christian liberty originated the saying so often to be met with in his letters: 'Keep

your heart in peace.' That is to say: Beware of hurry, anxiety, and bitterness of heart. These he called the ruin of devotion. He was even unwilling that people should meditate upon the great truths of Death, Judgment and Hell, unless they at the same time reassured themselves by the remembrance of God's love for them . . . The one point on which he chiefly insisted was that we must fear God from love, not love God from fear. 'To love Him from fear,' he used to say, 'is to put gall into our food and to quench our thirst with vinegar; but to fear Him from love is to sweeten aloes and wormwood.'[5]

Some of the pithy and most quoted sayings attributed to de Sales are found only in Camus' account. 'You can catch more flies with a spoonful of honey than you can with a barrel of vinegar', or 'The truth which is not charitable springs from a charity that is not true', or 'We must fear God out of love and not love him through fear', are perhaps not the Savoyard's exact words but they certainly capture his teaching on a world of hearts won to God's own heart through gentleness and charity.[6]

Beyond widely circulated portraits such as Goulu's, Charles Auguste de Sales', Camus' and Caussin's, the rendering of the beloved Savoyard that is perhaps the most telling is that crafted by Jane de Chantal herself. In 1627 she appeared at a first canonisation inquiry (at which her own brother André Frémyot, Archbishop of Bourges, and Jean-Pierre Camus were both present) on behalf of her dear friend. The inquiry lasted an entire week. Jane had carefully compiled her reminiscences according to a series of fifty-five questions compiled by the ecclesiastical court. The picture that emerged from her deposition is memorable. Drawing upon her own collection of Francis' letters addressed to herself as well as a letter she had written to Jean Goulu when he was compiling his *Life* of the Savoyard,[7] Jane's portrait, although shaped by the questions she was asked to address, strikes one as more intimate and revealing than, for example, Caussin's, who directed his authorised efforts towards memorialising the bishop as an heroic reformer, exemplary churchman and missionary. On her friend as one who conformed himself to God's will, Jane reported:

> ... I have always known the Blessed to be completely resigned to God's will, depending on it absolutely and unreservedly; nothing that could possibly happen to him, he used to say, would ever make him give up his firm resolution to accept willingly whatever God decided to do with him, or with anyone or anything connected with him.
>
> About five weeks after the Visitation was founded I got a fever, and as I was very ill my life was despaired of. When I was at this pass the Blessed came to see me and said: 'Maybe all God wants is our attempt and the good will we put into getting our little company ready for him, just as all he wanted was Abraham's willingness to sacrifice his son. If he wants us to turn back now we've just set out on a road, very well then, his will be done.' Now I can truly say that this was an act of heroic resignation because he foresaw that our way of life would bear much fruit for souls ...[8]

Jane's account here stresses Francis' graceful resignation to the will of God's good pleasure and highlights his ability to live with ease between the 'the two wills of God'. Her testimony on God's will continues in the same vein, using his family experience as an example.

> He saw his father die and two of his brothers, men greatly mourned and whose death he felt deeply; then a sister of his died and also a sister-in-law. When his mourning was at its most intense he said, like the Psalmist: 'I will be silent, O Lord, and not open my mouth, because this comes from you.' After his mother died, whom he loved as himself, and when he had closed her eyes and given her the last kiss of peace at the very moment of her passing, his heart swelled and he wept more than he had ever wept since his ordination, but without any bitterness, for

although he felt it very keenly, it was a peaceful sorrow. 'Like David I said: "I will be silent, O Lord, and not open my mouth, because this comes from you. Of course, if it had not been God's doing I would have cried out aloud at this blow, but as it is, I dare not cry out or disapprove, because after all, this comes from a Father's hand, and one which I have loved tenderly from my childhood, thanks to his goodness." ' Another time he said to me: 'Deep down in my heart of flesh and blood I feel this loss keenly, and yet I'm very much aware of a certain sweet peace, my spirit resting gently in divine providence, and this makes me very happy in spite of my grief.'[9]

This personal testimony by his dear friend perhaps brings the reader closer to the heart of the man Francis than some of the very public presentations of him by others. But it was not Jane's testimony that secured the bishop's lasting reputation as much as those of his other panegyrists and, most importantly, his own writings.[10]

As for Jane herself, she too was lionised by those who knew her.[11] Not atypical is the account left by Jeanne Chézard de Matel (1596–1670), visionary and foundress of the Sisters of the Incarnate Word. As a laywoman in Roanne, Mme de Matel was familiar with the newly founded Visitation Order and had once met the Visitation foundress herself. In a letter written from Lyons early in 1642, she reported to a Jesuit acquaintance that in August of the previous year she had learned that Jane was passing through Lyons on her way to Moulins. At that time she had a premonition that Jane would soon die (in fact she did die in December). Later that year, Jeanne de Matel dreamed she was in a Visitation church where a person clothed in white presented her with instruments of the Lord's Passion. The person, she reported, was 'Saint' Jane, whom she believed was now with God and praying for the establishment of the Incarnate Word community. On several other occasions of significance she reported feeling the spiritual presence of Mother de Chantal and in two instances, she experienced symbolic visions related to the Visitation and to Jane, who she believed to be 'in glory'.[12] The foundress loomed large in the religious imagination of her contemporaries.

Chief among Jane's more formal, less anecdotal, portraitists was her own secretary and great niece, Françoise-Madeleine de Chaugy, who had been tutored by her great aunt as a novice Visitandine.[13] Mother de Chaugy had a literary flair, was long an intimate of Jane and understood through personal practice the spirit of the early Visitation. Thus her portrait, though not a modern biography, is wonderfully authentic and revealing. The Chaugy memoir was divided into three segments that treat of Jane's life in the world, her life in religion and her virtues. The memoir's great virtue is that it contains many of Jane's own words as well as revealing anecdotes from her life.

What emerges is a portrait of a woman possessed of a singular capacity for giving of herself. A constant theme that runs through the narrative is the continual abandonment to God that she practised. Not only did Jane outlive many of those dear to her – her husband, three of her four children, her brother and father, her friend Francis, and the original founding members of the Visitation – but she was called upon for decades to cope with the arduous business of creating the legal and customary structures of a new religious institute. She had gifts for administration but no natural love for it. In addition, she struggled throughout her life with inner doubts. Always, in Chaugy's account, Jane turned in great simplicity and trust to the mercy of God. Abandonment to the will of God was her constant refrain. Her experience on the night before her entry into the new Visitation community is representative. She had prepared for this moment for years, prayerfully discerning God's will for her life, settling her own and her children's estates, undertaking the monumental legal and personal tasks of leave-taking from her home town. Then in the depth of the night she was seized with a terror that this great step was a mistake. She could not be worthy, everything to which her life had pointed was a lie. She had somehow deceived her spiritual director. Her father and father-in-law and her children would cry out to God for vengeance against her. Struggling against the ferocity of these terrors she

> . . . made a perfect act of abandonment of herself and all things, into God's hands. 'I remember well,' she said one time while speaking of this temptation, that 'I was healed by offering these words: My God, cast the eyes of your mercy on my nothingness, I abandon myself forever to your Providence; . . . my only interest in time and in eternity, is to obey and serve your majesty alone.' These words being offered with a sincere and loving heart, our Blessed Mother not only was restored to her earlier tranquility but [was granted] totally new joy and strength . . .'[14]

Because Jane herself wrote only out of necessity – letters and documents required for the ordering of the institute – the Chaugy memoir is especially valuable. It was first available for public circulation in a slightly adapted form through the efforts of Count Henry de Maupas du Tour, Bishop of Le Puy.[15] The Maupas du Tour version appeared only three years after Jane's death. The reputation of the mother-foundress was also carried within the Visitation community by oral tradition. The picture one forms from the Chaugy record is of a remarkable and passionate woman, drawn by the love of God to live deeply into the vision of a world of hearts. No less ardent and committed than her spiritual mentor and friend, Jane was nevertheless less innately buoyant, more hidden, and more mysterious to history.

THE LITERARY LEGACY

Without a doubt it is Francis de Sales' own *Introduction to the Devout Life* that is primarily responsible for his remarkable and long-lived influence. During his lifetime he wrote several versions: a hastily- assembled first draft was completed between 1607 and 1608 in the midst of his busy schedule by reworking a series of memos he had written to a number of devout women such as Louise Chastel, Madame de Charmoisy.

These women were the 'Dear Philothea' of the Introduction's preface, the many 'lovers of God' who flocked to the bishop's sermons and sought his guidance on how to live devoutly in the midst of their busy lives as wives, mothers and gentlewomen with responsibilities in society. As his episcopal responsibilities allowed, the busy shepherd reworked the draft into an amplified five-part version in 1610. In subsequent years he was to refine the *Introduction* even more to produce in 1619 the form familiar to generations of readers. Such was the hunger for this work that in between publication of these versions, rogue editions appeared throughout France and unauthorised translations showed up in Italy, England, Flanders and Spain.

Once the 1619 version appeared, publication became more standardised. By the end of the nineteenth century it is estimated that over four hundred editions of the work had appeared.[16] In England alone, both recusant Catholic versions and expurgated Protestant versions (with references to the Eucharist and 'popish' practices removed) circulated widely. Even King James I owned a richly bound and jewelled copy of the book, sent to him during de Sales' lifetime by Marie de Medici, widow of France's Henri IV, the monarch who had been so impressed by Bishop de Sales' preaching at Paris. James himself, having read the *Introduction* and carried it around with him for several weeks, expressed a desire to meet the gifted author.[17] In part, it was the current vogue for vernacular translations of edifying books encouraged by the Christian humanist agenda of the day that gave rise to these many editions. But the publication rate of the *Introduction* long outlived the humanist culture of Francis' era. Rather, the merits of the small volume itself must be seen as responsible for its popularity.

What is it about the *Introduction to the Devout Life* that has so captured the imagination of diverse readers in diverse countries across centuries and denominational divides? In the words of a twentieth-century Jesuit interpreter, 'The *Introduction à la Vie Dévote* for a long time served as the breviary for

Christians who, unable or unwilling to leave the world, aspired to live their baptismal faith with fervor.'[18]

Although he claimed no originality in his teaching, Francis presented traditional advice about the spiritual life in such a way as to adapt it to the circumstances of laypeople. In this he anticipated by three hundred years the 'universal call to holiness' proclaimed at Vatican II.

> Those who have written about devotion have nearly all had in mind the instruction of persons completely separated from life in the world. At least, they have taught a kind of devotion leading to such a complete separation. My purpose is to instruct people living in towns, the married, and those at princely courts. These are obliged by their state of life to lead an ordinary life to all outward appearances. Very often such persons do not want even to think of venturing on the devout life, finding an excuse in the false claim that it is impossible.
>
> These people are of the opinion no one caught up in the rush of living in the world should reach out for the palm of Christian devotion. But I want to make them understand that, just as the pearl oysters live in the sea without letting in a single drop of salt water, . . . and . . . a certain insect can fly about in the fire without burning its wings, so anyone with courage and determination can live in the world without being tainted by its spirit, finding springs of the fresh water of devotion in the world's salty waves and able to fly amid the flames of the temptations of the world without losing the wings of the holy desires of a devout life.[19]

This lay adaptation of the spiritual heritage in no way vitiated the core of the Christian spiritual life; the cultivation of a life transfigured by the Spirit of Christ remained the goal. However, this transformation was not to be accomplished primarily through external practices but through a deep interiority. The heart of the person was to be opened to the living, transforming divine presence. She or he was to 'Live

Jesus!' Always, this opening was a matter of Love's movements. To convey this truth Francis employed the image of engraving.

> In brief, men in love with a human and natural love have their thoughts turned, almost always, towards the person they love. Their heart is full of affection for her. They always speak her praises. In her absence, they lose no opportunity to express their love through letters. They carve her name on the bark of every tree they find. Similarly, those who love God cannot stop thinking of Him, seeking Him, longing for Him and speaking of Him. They would engrave, if it were possible, the holy and sacred name of Jesus on the breast of every person in the world.[20]

Francis' ability to capture the profound truths of the spiritual life in language with which his readers could identify was striking. His effort was directed not simply towards popularisation but towards expressing, in attractive and attracting ways, the truth that all love is from and ultimately for God. In the Salesian world, one does not have two hearts, one that loves God and one that loves others, but one heart created by and for God and the full realisation of God's designs throughout creation. All loves, if rightly ordered, are seen as capable of leading a person deeper into the mystery of divine love. For love and its motions are both means and end. In the cultivation of affectionate God-conscious relationships – marriage and family, community life, friendships – the living presence of Love is enfleshed in the world. *Vive Jésus!* Live Jesus!

The *Introduction* is a manual, accessible to beginners as well as rewarding for those proficient in the spiritual life, which directs the heart of the layperson towards Love's designs. In the spirit of Ignatius' *Spiritual Exercises*, by which the young Francis had been formed, 'Philothea' is introduced to a series of meditations on the goodness of God and the misery of human sin that elicit a resolution to choose and pursue a devout life, a life given over to love. Following this, she is introduced to various methods of prayer and devotional exercises, including partaking in the sacraments. Perhaps the most distinctively Salesian of these methods (and expressed in a uniquely Salesian way) is what the bishop calls the 'fashioning of a spiritual bouquet' at the end of a period of meditation as a means of deeply integrating what has been gleaned in prayer.

> You must gather a little devotional bouquet. This is what I mean. Those who have been walking in a beautiful garden do not willingly depart without gathering in their hands four or five flowers to smell and keep for the rest of the day. Thus ought we, when our soul has been entertaining itself and meditating on some mystery, to select one or two or three of those points in which we have found most relish and which are most proper for our advancement, to think frequently on them, and to smell them spiritually during the course of the day.[21]

The third segment of the *Introduction* concerns the practice of the virtues. Those distinctive 'little virtues' so dear to the hearts of the Salesian founders are highlighted and described as they might be practised in Philothea's circumstances. These little virtues all flow from charity itself. In his charming manner, Francis illustrates this,

> The king of bees never goes abroad into the fields without being surrounded by all his little subjects, and charity never enters the heart without lodging there all the other virtues in its train, exercising and disciplining them as a captain does his soldiers. It neither employs them all at the same time nor in every place . . . Occasions are not often presented for the exercise of fortitude, magnanimity and great generosity but meekness [gentleness], temperance, modesty and humility are virtues wherewith all the actions of our life should be tempered. There are other virtues more excellent than these, but nevertheless the practice of these last is more necessary. Sugar is more agreeable than salt, but the use of salt is more frequent and widespread.[22]

Some of his most cogent and subtle spiritual advice Francis offers in this section on the virtues. Gentleness towards others is to be accompanied by gentleness towards self. Poverty of spirit must be maintained in the midst of affluence, and richness of spirit amidst financial deprivation. Especially, he emphasises inward humility that he carefully distinguishes from a feigned self-abasement meant to attract praise or sympathy. And he counsels that life itself and the particular conditions of one's 'state in life' will no doubt supply all the humbling experiences one could ever invent for oneself.

Within this general discussion of the virtues Francis locates his advice about friendship and about married love. As has been suggested, friendship, especially spiritual friendship, was of supreme importance in the Savoyard's mind. To surround oneself with persons whose hearts are aflame with God's love is essential to the exercise of the heart in love, just as it is imperative to avoid persons who pursue relationships for self-serving or seductive purposes. This he felt was especially important for laypeople.

> ... [F]or those who dwell in the world, and desire to embrace true virtue, it is necessary to unite themselves together by a holy and sacred friendship. By this means they encourage, assist, and conduct one another to good deeds ... to secure and assist one another amidst the many dangerous passages through which they are to pass.[23]

Remarkably, and very progressively for the time in which he lived, Francis treated marriage as first and foremost a union of friends. While the procreation of children and the fashioning of a 'nursery of Christianity' was an essential part of the sacrament of marriage, in typical Salesian fashion the *Introduction* taught that it is the interior quality of any person or relationship that is crucial. The mutual love of spouses, an 'indissoluble union of hearts', was placed above the rearing of children in order of marital significance. This union should be based on a shared passion for God and sustained by gestures of affection.

> Love and fidelity joined together always produce familiarity and confidence. This is why the saints have used many reciprocal caresses in their married life, caresses truly affectionate, but chaste, tender and sincere ... The great St Louis, equally rigorous to his own flesh and tender in the love of his wife, was almost blamed for the abundance of such caresses. Actually, he rather deserved praise for being able to bring his martial and courageous spirit to stoop to these little duties so requisite for the preservation of conjugal love.[24]

The last two sections of the *Introduction* consider remedies against temptations; subtle inner temptations such as sadness, anxiety, discouragement, vanity, envy, jealousy and flirtation, as well as the very real exterior seductions that life in affluent European circles afforded. The text closes with practical exercises such as the examination of conscience, considerations on God's love, and resolutions that confirm one in the devout life.

Other writings of Francis de Sales were translated and circulated after his death.[25] The *Treatise on the Love of God*, his most ambitious work and the one most illustrative of his entire spiritual vision, was translated into Italian, English, Spanish, German, Polish and Latin during the seventeenth and eighteenth centuries. His *Entretiens spirituals*, or *Conferences*, also circulated in various uncritical editions. These were transcriptions of the familiar little talks that Francis gave to the Visitation sisters at the Gallery House, their first home. In pleasant weather, the small band would gather under the trees in the tiny orchard behind the house to hear their beloved founder speak about the essential inner spirit of their life together: obedience, confidence, abandonment, modesty, cordiality and simplicity, as well as more practical themes such as the Rule and the reception and profession of members. However, neither the *Conferences* nor the *Treatise* ever reached the vast popularity or wide audience of the *Introduction*. It is this last writing for which he is most remembered.

Jane de Chantal's literary legacy never matched that of her friend. Her writing style, which she self-consciously kept simple and unadorned as a practice of the virtue of simplicity, was not intended for the public eye. She produced no literary analogue to de Sales' *Introduction* or *Treatise*. She wrote solely in her capacities as administrator and spiritual mentor to the community of the Visitation. Most of her writing remained in circulation only within the Order. Nevertheless, a collection of her letters was compiled by Visitandine Marie-Aimée de Blonay and appeared in Lyons in 1644, just three years after Jane's death. These missives give some insight into the deeply maternal care that Jane lavished on her daughters in religion. What might have been an even more revealing source, Jane's correspondence with Francis de Sales, has unfortunately been lost to history. At his death, Jane was entrusted with his papers and, while she scrupulously preserved his missives for posterity, in a gesture of what is assumed to be humility, she burned all the letters she had sent to him that he had collected over the years. Nevertheless, a significant correspondence with other people remained and was finally, at the end of the twentieth century, published in a critical edition.[26]

CONTINUING INFLUENCE

This combination of the wide circulation and continued publication of de Sales' writing, the continuing influence of the Visitation and the enduring memory of the Salesian founders, both anecdotal and through the circulation of their *Lives*, kept the Salesian vision of a world of hearts before the Christian community throughout the seventeenth and eighteenth and into the early nineteenth centuries. Francis de Sales and Jane de Chantal became members of that cadre of holy ones held close in the Christian imagination. It is probably safe to say that those who held the Salesian founders in highest esteem, outside of the regions of Savoy and southeastern France where the friends were claimed as local heroes, were educated people and the hierarchy of the Catholic world. In fact, their reputations were greatly enhanced by the very currency of the type of holiness they exemplified.

Wonderworkers, martyrs and healers from the earliest times had captured the popular Christian imagination and been proclaimed by the faithful as saints. But as Christianity developed and centralised in the Middle Ages, the official process of naming saints to be venerated on the universal church calendar came more and more under the control of the ecclesiastical hierarchy. Early modern Catholicism, the era of Jane and Francis' flourishing, took seriously the process of saint-making. During that time the Bolandists, a group of Jesuit scholars, began a project to record and edit sources related to the lives of saints, thus bringing modern canons of historical interpretation to the saint-making process.[27] The values of that vibrant, militant early modern church were reflected in the paradigms of holiness that it held up for admiration.[28] Founders of new orders, reformers of existing religious orders, exemplary bishops, champions of Catholic orthodoxy, and missionary saints were in vogue. While earlier models of sanctity – martyrs, monastics, visionaries, wonderworkers, ascetics – were not forgotten, those who were granted ecclesial recognition during the years surrounding the Salesian tradition's founding were definitely in the heroic mould promoted by the Catholic hierarchy. Between 1570 and 1770 twenty-seven men and five women were canonised. All were either bishops, priests or members of religious orders. Half of these newly-minted saints hailed from the new orders created during the era of reform, another quarter were reformers of older orders. Jane and Francis fit the model of sanctity promoted after the Council of Trent. As a bishop he was represented as implementing the vision and decrees of a newly-energised Tridentine Catholicism. As a missionary he defended and promoted the faith seen as true. As a foundress, she represented the revitalisation and reaffirmation of religious life that the Catholic reform promoted.

During the Salesian founders' lifetimes the aura of sanctity clung to them and at their deaths their remains, as was the custom, were viewed as relics. Francis was formally beatified in 1661 and canonised in 1665.[29] Jane was recognised somewhat later. Her beatification took place in 1751 and her canonisation in 1767. Inevitably, in the process of translating the complex reality of a human life to iconic status for universal emulation – no matter how grace-filled it might be – a certain flattening takes place. Jane and Francis were identified with specific virtues and held up in each successive age as patrons for changing causes. For example, the nineteenth century, that era of a Church much ravaged by the French Revolution and beleaguered by the rising rationalism and scientism of the modern world, saw in Bishop de Sales primarily a great champion of Catholic orthodoxy and emphasised the missionary period of his life. It was in this era, in 1877, that Pope Pius IX proclaimed him Doctor of the Church.

In addition, subsequent biographies sometimes had the effect of fixing in collective memory a certain, not always balanced, image of the Salesian founders. This is especially true in Jane de Chantal's case. A successful full-length biography of her, published in 1863 by Émile Bougaud, Bishop of Laval, contrasted her character to that of the gentle Francis de Sales and portrayed her as the firm, heroic, strong, even formidable one of the pair. The idea of Jane as the *femme forte*, as well as the image of her as the sort of single-minded woman who would walk over the body of her son still lingers to this day. This is not a balanced view as it ignores all evidence of her maternal tenderness both with her own children and her daughters in religion, and her capacity for deep and long-lasting friendships.[30]

While the esteemed bishop was most remembered for his contributions to a renewed Church, he was not entirely without recognition as a posthumous miracle worker. When in 1632 reports circulated of the demonic possession of Jeanne des Anges, Abbess of the Ursuline convent in Loudun, national attention was riveted. Eventually seventeen nuns of the community were afflicted by seizures and contortions and an exorcist, Jesuit Jean-Joseph Surin, was called in. After a long-drawn-out drama, during which Surin periodically collapsed from the stress, the possessed Abbess experienced a healing through the intercession of the Savoyard saint. The final exorcism was effected by a pilgrimage to the tomb of Francis de Sales in Annecy arranged by the highest authorities and applauded by the French Queen and cardinals alike.

CONTINUING INFLUENCE: THE FRENCH SCHOOL

Less dramatic, but more profound, was Francis de Sales' incalculable influence on the spiritual and theological ethos of subsequent generations. This impact, and the impact of Jane through the Order of the Visitation, was immense. Seen most immediately from hindsight is the Salesian contribution to the currents of spirituality that flourished in France in the late seventeenth century, currents that were to have incalculable influence in the Catholic world in the following two centuries.

Pierre de Bérulle, founder of the French or Bérullian School of spirituality, was Francis' contemporary and the two admired each other from the time of their early contact at the Acarie salon in Paris. Despite that contact and the Jesuit training they both received, the two men in fact worked from fairly distinct theological premises and developed discreet teachings. Bérulle's thought is marked by its theocentrism, its guarded view of human capabilities, its mystical Christocentrism encouraged by the practice of 'adherence' to the 'states' of Jesus, its Mariological emphasis and its exaltation of the priesthood. Many of the giants of French Catholic renewal during the later part of the *grand siècle* were shaped by Bérulle's spiritual vision. While the French School of spirituality is a parallel one, Salesian influence upon it is significant and recognised by scholars.[31] The Savoyard and his French colleague, whatever their differing theological anthropologies and emphases (Bérulle was critical of Francis' optimism),[32] did share a common passion for the reform of the Church. In fact, it was Francis' enthusiasm for the Italian Oratory founded by Philip Neri and his desire to found a similar institution for the spiritual renewal of the priesthood in Savoy that inspired Bérulle to establish the French Oratory. Francis never succeeded in his dream but Bérulle did, and the Congregation of the Oratory in Paris and its daughter houses throughout France became the cradle for a priesthood devoted to the spread of a reformed Catholicism through the vehicle of internal missions.[33]

The later-born luminaries of the French School, Charles de Condren, Jean-Jacques Olier and John Eudes, were definitely Bérulle's spiritual sons but they also breathed the air that the Salesian spirit had fully permeated. To begin with, all parties shared the mutually edifying recognition of common engagement in the Church's work of renewal. Charles de Condren, Bérulle's successor as superior of the Oratory, was also a member of the Acarie circle and was admired by the Salesian founders. Jane de Chantal was to write of him that he was capable of teaching the angels.[34] Olier, nurtured at the French Oratory and later founder of his own seminaries and the Society of St Sulpice (Sulpicians), which was dedicated to the purpose of providing seminary-directors, knew the mature Francis de Sales as a child. The boy developed a deep veneration for the older prelate who had visited the Olier home in Lyons, and a 1622 blessing by him had confirmed the youth in his vocation to religious life. This veneration was passed down to Olier's spiritual sons well into the nineteenth century.

John Eudes, the youngest of the quartet of French School luminaries, not only esteemed the Salesian founders but his own spiritual vision owes a greater debt to them than do the visions of his older compatriots.[35] Eudes was the founder of several communities dedicated to the renewal of the priesthood and the wider church: the Society of Jesus and Mary (Eudists) and the Congregation of Our Lady of Charity of the Refuge. He was also a product of the French Oratory. An indefatigable preacher (during his life he preached no fewer than 110 missions throughout France), he believed, like de

Sales, that his listeners could be drawn to the love of God 'heart to heart'. In fact, Eudes had a profound devotion to the hearts of both Mary and Jesus.[36] The image of the Heart of Jesus, while not uncommon in popular devotion and long promoted for private use by a number of religious communities, was carried in Eudist tradition not so much as a visual image but as an overarching metaphor. This was the language of the devout life – the life of heart to heart – as envisioned by Francis de Sales. We know that John Eudes read the *Treatise on the Love of God*, and Salesian expressions such as 'Live Jesus!' and 'Jesus, King of Hearts' are found throughout the younger man's *Kingdom of Jesus*. Moreover, while Bérulle and others in the French School spoke of 'religion', Eudes followed his Savoyard predecessor by employing the term 'devotion' when referring to the practice of the Christian spiritual life. Indeed, Francis de Sales' thought was often echoed in such phrases as 'the first Christians were said to have only one heart and one soul'. Eudes' pastoral sensitivities as well as his own spiritual tastes allowed him to emphasise the love of God through the metaphor of the heart. It was he who wrote the first office and Mass for the liturgical celebration of the Heart of Jesus that was celebrated in 1672. His affective approach owes much to his internalisation of the Salesian spirit.

That spirit was breathed in the France of John Eudes not only through de Sales' ever-popular writings but through the ever-present community of the Visitation. By Jane de Chantal's death there were over eighty monasteries in existence, the vast majority of them in France and Savoy. One example from Eudes' life, among many others that might be cited, concerns the preacher's dependence on the Visitation as he attempted to found his own women's community.[37] Among the ills of society he considered pressing was the plight of women forced into prostitution. In 1641, he opened a shelter for 'penitent women' and entrusted its care to a group of charitable ladies. But the arrangement did not flourish and many of the caretakers left the work. To establish a solid community foundation and form the novices who entered, Eudes called upon members of the Visitation monastery in Normandy. Although involvement in such an active apostolate was hardly the explicit charism of the Visitation, the well-respected sisters' services were sought in such cases. Eudes' Congregation of Our Lady of Charity of the Refuge thus owes its existence to the Visitation, in whose spirit the active religious were formed.[38] Earlier, Jane de Chantal herself had assumed responsibility for a group of Parisian penitents. The Paris Visitation directed this work until 1677 when it was taken over by the Refuge Sisters.

CONTINUING INFLUENCE: THE VINCENTIAN SCHOOL

Francis and Jane were not only claimed as mentors and allies by the French School, they were emulated in that other great seventeenth-century French spiritual tradition, the Vincentian. Vincent de Paul, known to later generations as the apostle to the poor, was a slightly younger contemporary of Francis de Sales. Vincent's contact with the Savoyard was critical in his own spiritual maturation. The two first met in 1618 and a deep mutual regard sprang up between them. Francis' irenic and charitable pastoral approach struck the feisty Vincent de Paul as enviable and set the stage for his own spiritual transformation. Moody by temperament, Vincent prayed to be delivered from his melancholy. With Francis' example before him, eventually the younger man developed a gentler style.[39] The two spiritual giants maintained contact throughout de Sales' lifetime.

Vincent's conferences to his Daughters of Charity, a simple congregation devoted to the performance of the works of mercy among the poor, contain many references to the Bishop of Geneva's work and words. The *Introduction to the Devout Life* was touted thus . . . 'whoever would exactly observe everything contained in this book would attain great perfection, although it would appear that all practices recommended are ordinary and accommodated to human weakness'. Vincent compared the spirituality of the *Introduction* to the Daughters' Rule of Life.[40] To the new priests formed in Vincent's male community, the Congregation of Priests for the Mission (Vincentians or Lazarists), the founder taught the practice of mental prayer 'according to the method of our blessed father, the bishop of Geneva'.[41] So consonant were the spiritual ideals of the Vincentian and Salesian families that after Francis died, Vincent succeeded his late friend as Spiritual Father of the Visitation in Paris and became spiritual director to Jane de Chantal herself.

The web of Salesian-Vincentian interconnection in this era of spiritual renewal included Louise de Marillac, Vincent's long-term colleague and co-founder of the Daughters of Charity. Even before she met Vincent de Paul, Louise had been nurtured on the contemporary crop of popular spiritual writers including Francis de Sales. During a period of profound crisis before she was widowed, Louise had received the grace of an inner assurance that God would allow her some day to make religious profession. This grace she believed came from Francis de Sales, the man whom she esteemed during his lifetime and had even hoped would be her own spiritual confidant.[42] While this desire was never realised, in her later direction of the Daughters of Charity, Louise drew upon Francis' *Introduction* when developing retreat material for her community.[43] And throughout her life Louise sought the intercession of the Savoyard saint. A 1630 manuscript recording her resolutions from Ascension to Pentecost include the intention

> ... to mortify myself interiorly and exteriorly insofar as I am able. To offer to God, several times each day, the charity which he put into the heart of the Blessed Francis de Sales and to ask, through the intercession of this saint, that the designs of the holy will of God may be fulfilled in me.[44]

Thus, although they were on the early cusp of the renewal of French Catholicism, Francis de Sales and Jane de Chantal's spirit was very much alive throughout the seventeenth century and their exemplary lives would continue to shape Christian spirituality into the eighteenth and early nineteenth centuries.

CONTINUING INFLUENCE: RAYMOND BONAL AND THE PRIESTS OF THE VISITATION OF HOLY MARY

A less well-known but fascinating case of Salesian influence involves one Raymond Bonal (1600–1653).[45] Bonal, an indefatigable preacher, teacher, writer and reform-minded priest, came to maturity at the end of Francis' life: the Bishop of Geneva died just two years before Bonal's own ordination to the priesthood. Despite the fact that they never met, the elder man's reputation and spirit were never far from the younger churchman's mind. De Sales had held the reform of the clergy close to his heart but was never able to realise his dream of establishing a community for priests. By the time of Bonal's ordination, Bérulle's French Oratory, dedicated to the theological, moral and spiritual revivification of the secular clergy, was well established in the country. Bonal was closely tied to the second superior of the French Oratory, Charles de Condren. But it was Monseigneur de Génève who held pride of place in Bonal's heart: the late bishop's unfinished dream haunted him. During his youthful studies with the Jesuits of Cahors, and his time spent with the Secular Priests of Christian Doctrine (Doctrinaires) in his hometown of Villefranche, Raymond had often heard tales of the heroic reformers, Charles Borromeo and Francis de Sales, and he had been imbued with the teachings of the recent Council of Trent that promoted clerical reform.

Consciously modelling himself on the man he referred to as 'Saint' Francis (de Sales would not be officially canonised until 1665), Bonal went about his pastoral duties with zeal, catechising, preaching, directing souls, hearing confessions, and promoting reform. It was rumoured among his contemporaries that he had such a gift of persuasion that what had been said of Francis de Sales could be said of Bonal: that having preached in a village, he brought great good but also ill because he had spoiled the residents for all subsequent preachers.[46]

While ministering to the inhabitants of the town of Villefranche during the pestilence of 1630, Bonal confided to two colleagues his dream of establishing a community of parish priests that would live according to the spirit of Francis de Sales. Soon his dream began to materialise. He was given the oversight of the Church of Notre-Dame de Treize Pierres in Villefrance with the understanding that priests of holy life and sound doctrine would gather there. Despite the deaths of his first companions, Bonal became convinced that he was called to found a community under Francis' aegis which would imitate the saint's zeal in the Chablais missions, especially in neglected parishes where faith was lax. It was not only the late bishop's missionary zeal that Raymond admired, but his method. One must hate the heresy but love the heretic, Francis had taught, and through his affable, courteous conversations and his unfailing efforts to communicate heart to heart, Francis had succeeded in converting a prominent lawyer in Thonon. This was the method and the spirit with which Bonal longed to imbue the priests of his dreamt-of community.

In the spring of 1635, Bonal embarked on a pilgrimage to the Salesian holy sites. His compass was set towards Annecy. On the way he stopped in Lyons and venerated the heart of the founder that was kept in a reliquary at the first monastery of the Visitation in that town.[47] In Savoy, he paid his respects to Francis' brother and successor, Bishop Jean-François de Sales. Finally he enjoyed several edifying conversations with Jane de Chantal herself at the Visitation monastery in Annecy. She confirmed Bonal's belief that Francis had hoped to found a priestly community for parish service. Bonal thus became, in his own and others' minds, a true son of the blessed bishop. His pilgrimage ended with a return visit to Jean-François de Sales, where Francis' vision of an institute was clarified and a blessing given. The institute, 'Priests of the Visitation of Holy Mary', was to model itself closely on the women's community that Jane and Francis had begun in 1610. Contact with Salesian spirituality continued as, when in Paris in 1636, Bonal visited the Visitation monasteries on Rue de St-Antoine and Rue-St-Jacques.[48]

Thus was founded the men's community that the Salesian founder had imagined. Both Jane and the second superior of Annecy, Mother de Blonay, in later years sent letters of 'family' support and blessing. 'Dear Father . . . your humility makes you a dear brother of the Visitation. I know, Monsieur, that you are a true son of our Blessed Father': thus wrote Mother de Blonay in 1643. So faithful was this favoured son to the spirit of the founder that he tried to duplicate the Rule of the Visitation in detail. This caused some difficulties, especially when he insisted that the community be under the direct control of the diocesan bishop, as was the Visitation. What worked well for an order of cloistered women was not always viable for a community of mobile men. Nevertheless, Bonal's absolute devotion to his mentor never waned. When in 1641 he preached a retreat to the Visitandines at Albi, the entire content of the preaching was drawn from the spirit and maxims of the Salesian founder. When one of the sisters expressed amazement at his grasp of Salesian principles, Bonal replied that he had been studying the master's works closely for over twenty years.[49]

Much of the remainder of Bonal's life was taken up with the further work of clerical renewal: the founding of seminaries, first in Villefranche then outside, notably in Toulouse. The history of the priestly community was chequered and eventually, after Bonal's death and varied changes of fortune, it merged with the Vincentian Congregation of the Mission. It would be left to the nineteenth-century heirs of the Salesian world of hearts to rekindle and found priestly congregations animated by Francis' vibrant spirit.

CONTINUING INFLUENCE: THEOLOGICAL CONTROVERSIES

Bonal was not alone in his desire to emulate and call upon Francis and Jane. Often in theological quarrels or contested issues that engaged the Church, the Salesian saints would re-emerge as witnesses or fall under suspicion. Such was the case in the last quarter of the seventeenth century during the Quietist controversy. The swirl of agitation around the doctrines of 'pure love' which eventually led to the condemnation of Madame Guyon and to the censure of the writings of her supporter, François Fénelon, Bishop of Cambrai, shows the ubiquitous influence of Salesian spirituality. In his 1697 *Maxims of the Saints* Fénelon often quoted Francis de Sales, especially Book IX of the *Treatise*. The Bishop of Cambrai looked to tradition to defend the idea of a 'pure love' of God held for God's sake alone, which involves no self-interest or voluntary deliberate desire. This teaching, he believed, was found in Francis de Sales' writings. The Savoyard's ideas inspired the younger bishop: Francis' emphasis on abandonment and 'holy indifference' in the response to the will of God's good pleasure was consonant with Fénelon's own spiritual posture.[50] Numerous images and references reveal Fénelon's dependence on Salesian thought.[51] Madame Guyon, in her turn, was greatly influenced by the Salesian saints. As a young woman, not only had she avidly read the *Introduction to the Devout Life*, but she was so moved by a life of Jane de Chantal that she hoped to enter the nearby Visitation convent at Montargis, a desire thwarted by an arranged marriage. Nevertheless, she continued to be inspired by Jane and consciously to model her life on that of the Visitation foundress.[52]

Interestingly, the great opponent of Fénelon and Guyon's brand of spiritual teachings, fabled orator Jacques Bénigne Bossuet, Bishop of Meaux, also quoted de Sales at length in his critique of Fénelon. Further, Bossuet's panegyrics on the Savoyard bishop who preceded him by a generation show the esteem in which that classical generation of churchmen held their Salesian forebearer.[53] Francis was for that generation a model of equilibrium, an example of personal zeal and rigour and a champion of the Church who sustained allegiance to the faith in the midst of a troubled world. As each age fits its heroes to its own image, so the late seventeenth and eighteenth century found in the Salesian spirit that which it could admire. Francis de Sales, ever optimistic, thus towered over an era suffused with theological pessimism fed by a rigorous Augustinianism. His joyous devotion, while in contrast to much of what his panegyrists taught, still excited their admiration. Salesian luminaries Francis and Jane continued to communicate heart to heart.

5. BEHOLD THIS HEART!: MARGARET MARY ALACOQUE AND THE SACRED HEART

... I had the good fortune of spending all day on the feast of the Visitation before the Blessed Sacrament. My sovereign showed me a very high place, spacious and wonderfully beautiful, in the midst of which was set up a throne of flames and within it the lovable Heart of Jesus with Its wound. From this shot forth flames so luminous and glowing that the whole place was lighted up and warmed by them. The Blessed Virgin was on one side and Saint Francis de Sales and the saintly Father de la Colombière on the other. The Daughters of the Visitation were there with their guardian angels beside them, each one holding a heart in hand . . . Our holy founder, speaking to his daughters, said to them: Esteemed daughters, come and draw from the source of all blessings the water of salvation . . . In this divine heart you will find an easy way of acquitting yourselves perfectly of what is enjoined you in the first article of your Directory . . . Let their whole life and endeavor tend to unite them with God . . . With this in view, let us pray in the Heart, and through the Heart of Jesus . . . Our good example shall consist in living in holy conformity with the holy maxims and virtues of this divine Heart . . .[1]

Margaret Mary Alacoque

The language of the heart is ubiquitous in the Salesian tradition.[2] Founders Francis de Sales and Jane de Chantal bequeathed to their followers a spiritual vision of a world of hearts. When in 1611, on the first anniversary of the founding of the Visitation, Francis wrote to his friend Jane he could claim: 'Truly our little congregation is the work of the Hearts of Jesus and Mary. The dying Savior has given birth to us through the opening of his Sacred Heart.'[3]

And when Jane years later wrote to her spiritual daughters she echoed his sentiment:

> Here I am back again to greet my very dear daughters whom I love with all my heart. You are, I hope, always striving more earnestly to rid yourselves of all that is displeasing to your sovereign spouse and to acquire those virtues which please him. Oh, my dearest sisters, how deeply is this wish engraved in my heart! . . . Show a child-like trust and gentleness toward one another . . . So, courage, dear ones. May all of you together, and each one in particular, work at this and never grow slack. May you all live in harmony with one heart and mind in God . . . If you imitate Him in all [your] little trials and make His divine will rule in you, He will fill it with every blessing . . . I urge you to this once again, for the love of our Savior and by his precious blood, and with the deep affection of my heart which is all yours in Jesus.[4]

But for the founders the heart was primarily a metaphor, a word picture that gave expression to a theological and spiritual vision. The actual visual imagery of the Sacred Heart of Jesus, which was to gain such prominence in Catholic circles in later centuries, was only a small part of the Salesian world of hearts. Yet it was a significant part.[5] The silver cross that each Visitation sister wore from the time she took vows, bore a central engraving of a pierced heart surmounted by the papal cross from which three drops of blood issued. Two letters – M and A for Mary – were flanked by small flames.[6] Beneath the cross were the three mountains of Calvary topped by a martyr's palm. In that same anniversary letter of 10 June 1611, Francis communicated his inspiration for the coat of arms that would herald the community to the world. He sent a messenger bearing the letter to Jane, 'his very dear daughter' and 'dear mother':

> ... the thought that God gave to me this night [was] that our Visitation house is, by God's grace, noble and important enough that it should have its own coat of arms, blazon, and motto. Therefore, my dear Mother, if you agree, I think that we should take for our coat of arms a single heart pierced with two arrows, enclosed in a crown of thorns, and surmounted by a cross. This poor heart will be engraved with the sacred names of Jesus and Mary.[7]

These various visual representations of the heart were woven into the fabric of Visitation life and gave material expression to the Salesian world of hearts. It would be left to a late seventeenth-century Visitandine from the monastery at Paray-le-Monial – Margaret Mary Alacoque (1647–1690) – to give voice to a full-fledged devotion to the heart of Jesus, a devotion that would be taken up and spread throughout the universal Catholic Church.[8]

In the lore of the Visitation, it is deemed significant for the development of Sacred Heart devotion that Francis' letter was written on the Friday following the Feast of Corpus Christi, the very day on which, over sixty years later, Margaret Mary received a visitation from Jesus Himself. Her divine visitor would call for the institution of a feast honouring His Heart. In fact, Francis' description of the coat of arms, reproduced in a number of contexts over the years, bears a close resemblance to the visionary Sacred Heart that Margaret Mary later drew for veneration in the monastery novitiate.

Although it is sometimes suggested, Margaret Mary did not invent devotion to the Sacred Heart. Nor were Francis de Sales and Jane de Chantal before her alone in using the heart as a central image for the Christian spiritual life (although no one else used the image in such a foundational and wide-ranging way).[9] Christian language of the heart can be traced back to the patristic era and the early Church fathers' interpretation of scripture. They saw the pierced side of Christ, with its issue of water and blood (John 19:34), as an allegory of the Church with its living streams of baptism and Eucharist. The pierced side was a cleft in the rock from which the fountain of life poured forth (John 7:37–38; Isaiah 53:5; 1 Cor. 10:4; Song of Songs 2:14). The fathers saw the Church as born from the opened side, indeed, from the heart of Christ. Similarly, they seized upon the figure of John, the beloved disciple, who rested on the breast of Jesus (John 13:23–24) and conceived him to be the archetype of the contemplative, the one who is intimate with Christ's heart.

This allegorical speculation of the early fathers was amplified during the medieval era and gave way to an intensely personal piety that was cultivated mainly in monastic circles. Focus moved from the wounded Lord to the wounds themselves. The side wound became a special focus of cultic devotion. It became the symbol *par excellence* of the intimate, loving relationship between creator and creatures. A mysticism of the Heart developed as language from the Song of Songs became the interpretative lens through which the divine–human relationship was seen. The mystic, desiring union, would drink from the opened side, seek refuge inside the opened wound, and be incorporated into the divine through that bleeding portal. The portal itself was known as the gateway to the Heart. In that most intimate of chambers, the ultimate mysteries of divine love were explored. The true lover of the divine was a bride, a dove nestled in the cleft in the rock (Song of Songs 1:14; 4:9). By the thirteenth century women in the spiritual circle of the Rhineland monastery of Helfta – luminaries such as Gertrude the Great and Mechtilde of Hackborn – were receiving visions of Christ appearing to them to reveal his Heart.

Late medieval prayers, litanies, accounts of visions, drawings and woodcuts abound which have the wounds and Heart as their focus. Devotion to the wounded Heart was associated throughout the Middle Ages with the Cistercian, Benedictine, Franciscan, Dominican, and Carthusian religious orders.

During the fifteenth century the devotion spread beyond the orders to the emergent tradition of lay piety. By the sixteenth century the powerful new Society of Jesus (the Jesuits) had taken up devotion. Through these varied communities, the corpus of medieval mysticism, and the iconographic tradition, the devotion flowed into the confluence of streams that found a common streambed in the newly emergent Salesian tradition.

EARLY YEARS

Thus when Margaret Mary Alacoque entered the Visitation community of Paray-le-Monial in 1671, a deep history of devotion to the Heart of Jesus already existed. It was, however, a popular and private devotion, not one universally fostered and, interestingly, not one familiar to the Paray-le-Monial Visitation. In fact, the practices Margaret Mary was to introduce there were seen as a novelty. There were, however, contemporary indications that the devotion was becoming more systematised and theologically rooted at the close of the seventeenth century. John Eudes, founder of the Eudists and exponent of the French School of spirituality, ministered in the north of France quite distant from Paray in the south-central region. In 1668, Eudes developed the first Mass text for the Heart of Jesus and wrote the first theologically informed treatise on the devotion, *The Sacred Heart of Jesus*.[10] At the same time, members of the Society of Jesus were actively promoting devotion to the Heart.

Among them was Claude la Colombière (1641–1682) who in 1675 was assigned as confessor to the Visitation monastery at Paray. What he discovered among the little flock of nuns was a newly professed woman who confided in him the revelations she claimed to have received from Christ concerning the desires of His Sacred Heart. Margaret Mary came to that confidence somewhat painfully. She was young in the community and did not at first seem to fit in well. She had chosen religious life despite the objections of her family, and had entered with a lively sense of an ongoing interior relationship with her beloved Lord. Her childhood years had not been easy ones: her father's death had left the girl and her mother isolated and dependent on uncaring relatives. As a young woman, she had turned to Jesus for companionship and He led her to religious life. Indeed, she was on such familiar terms with Him that they carried on a continual conversation. At times, her colloquies distracted her from monastic observance. An oft-repeated story recalls her as a young religious assigned to keep watch over the community's animals so they would not wander into the vegetable garden. Margaret Mary fell into a rapture and the creatures ate the week's groceries. Only much later, after her revelations of the Sacred Heart were authenticated, did anyone recall such stories fondly. Until Claude la Colombière arrived on the scene the young Visitandine was regarded by some as a questionable community member, although several of the superiors under whom she lived came to value her particular gifts.

She spoke to her confessor of three particular revelations. Later in the year of his arrival she would receive a fourth. The first occurred in December 1672 on the Feast of John the Beloved Disciple, the one whom scripture said laid his head on the breast of his Lord as they reclined at supper (John 13:23–26). Margaret Mary was praying before the Eucharist, as was her wont, when she experienced being surrounded by the divine presence.

> He made me rest a long time on His divine breast where he showed me the marvels of his love and the unspeakable secrets of his Sacred Heart that had always been hidden before . . . He said, my divine Heart is so impassioned with love for humanity, and for you especially, it cannot contain the flames of its burning charity inside. It must spread them through you and show itself to humanity . . .[11]

During the encounter, the young Visitandine experienced a mystical 'exchange of hearts'. Jesus asked for her heart, placed it in His own and returned it to her as a burning heart-shaped flame. This token of His love was also to be a participation in

His suffering; the pain of it would always remain with her and she would become an active agent of suffering redemptive love in the world. Jesus then bestowed a new name upon her, 'Beloved Disciple of My Sacred Heart'. This first, initiatory, revelation would be followed by three more that expanded upon the mission with which she was entrusted. She was to promote the celebration of a Eucharist in honour of the Sacred Heart on the First Friday of every month. She was to encourage the observance of an hour of Eucharistic adoration on the night between Thursday and Friday in memory of Jesus' agony in the garden. Most significantly, she was to urge the institution of a yearly Feast of the Sacred Heart to be placed on the Friday following the liturgical Feast of Corpus Christi (the Body and the Blood of Christ).

There was a characteristic spiritual tone to these revelations; they emphasised the devotional postures of adoration and reparation. Adoration was due the divine Heart that loved humanity with such abandon yet had suffered so for that love. Margaret Mary identified the continuing suffering of the Heart with the laxity of religious life and with the disdain showed for the abundant graces of the Eucharist by those who rejected the sacrament or held that it should not often be frequented. Reparation was thus due to the despised Heart: the devotional practices the Visitandine outlined would lovingly 'repair' the damage done.

Hearing the report of his spiritual charge, Claude la Colombière became convinced that the revelations were authentic. The two religious heard in this divine communiqué a call. In June of 1675 they consecrated themselves to the Sacred Heart and the mission they believed was ordained for them. Despite these vows, the progress of the devotion was not smooth. Soon Fr Claude was transferred to England where, under recusant laws, he was persecuted. Weakened by his ordeal, he was to die in 1679. In her own community, Margaret Mary's ideas received a cautious reception. Novel devotions and extraordinary spiritual experiences were suspect, both in the Visitation and in the general spiritual climate of the time. At

the end of the seventeenth century, Visitandine life was idealised as simple and humble obedience to the community rule;
sisters were lauded to the extent that they could be seen as
'living rules'. The young professed visionary, always somewhat
unique, was scrutinised, and her humility was tested in many
ways.

Eventually, she was able to carry out her mission. In 1685
she was made novice mistress (a fact that indicates the extent
to which she had won the trust of the community) and in July
of that year an image of the Sacred Heart, replicating the
image she had seen in ecstasy and reminiscent of the heart on
the Visitation standard, was displayed and venerated by
novices and novice mistress. Thus began the devotion's gradual
progression. The spread was two-pronged, Visitandine and
Jesuit.[12]

EXPANSION OF THE DEVOTION

There were obstacles to overcome within the Paray community,
but gradually the practice moved out of the novitiate and
veneration of the Heart was accepted within the entire monastery. Plans developed to build a chapel in the garden for the
purpose of venerating the Sacred Heart in the manner pre-
scribed in Margaret Mary's visions. Paray-le-Monial became
the epicentre of the devotion's diffusion. Gradually, other Visitation monasteries adopted the practice; those within
geographical proximity of Paray and those in which a sister
was in correspondence with Margaret Mary were the first:
Autun, Dijon, Charolles, Moulins and Paris were among the
monasteries that soon promoted the devotion. It is significant
that the promotion became, not a private, but a communal,
undertaking 'occupying souls and space' within the Visitandine
world.[13] Chapels were built, paintings were commissioned feat-
uring the Salesian founders or, after her death, Margaret Mary.
Some of the chapels were inside the cloister and thus available
only to the nuns, but others were built alongside the monasteries and were open to the faithful. Indeed, lay donors came

forward to fund their construction. Eventually, confraternities of the Sacred Heart were established, enabling laypeople to engage in acts of adoration and reparation under the mantle of the Visitation Order. Meanwhile, the liturgical aspect of the devotion grew apace. Masses and litanies in honour of the Sacred Heart were composed by Visitation sisters and in varied locations feasts were celebrated.

The enthusiasm felt for the devotion and for the Lord at its centre was infectious. Writing to Jesuit father Jean Croiset in 1689, Margaret Mary would confide:

> This divine Heart is an inexhaustible fountain from which three streams are continually flowing. The first is the stream of mercy, which flows down upon sinners and brings the spirit of sorrow and repentance. The second is the stream of charity which brings relief to all those who are suffering under some need, and especially those who are striving for perfection. These will find, through the help of the holy angels, the means of overcoming their difficulties. The third is the stream of love and light for perfect friends whom He wills to unite with Himself . . . Moreover, this divine Heart will be a sure refuge and a harbor of safety at the hour of death for all those who have honored It during life. It will protect and defend them.
>
> I must mention something that occurred to me while writing to you. It is that this divine Heart is like a beautiful tree that has sent its roots down deep into the Order of the Visitation because of its lowliness. There its power and grandeur will appear more strikingly. This tree bears good and wholesome fruit of every kind which will counteract the poison of sin and give back life to the soul.[14]

The early Visitandine practice of electing superiors from another monastery meant that there was exchange among the varied houses. A superior from a community where the devotion was strong could promote it in her new position. By the time Margaret Mary died in 1690, the momentum for its propagation was strong. Tellingly, despite her active advocacy of the devotion after she was made novice mistress, Margaret Mary remained mute about the revelatory visions that were the devotion's source. It was only when Fr la Colombière's 1677 retreat notes were read aloud in the convent refectory, that the Paray community became aware that a visionary existed in their midst. Once they were convinced of the authenticity of the visions, her superiors encouraged Margaret Mary to record her experiences.[15] She would not have written her spiritual autobiography had it not been required by her confessor, Fr Rolin. In fact, when Rolin's term of office was completed and she was no longer under obedience to him, she stopped writing. But by that time, the devotion had taken on a life of its own beyond its beginnings.

JESUIT SUPPORT

With the Visitandines, the Jesuit fathers actively promoted the cult of the Sacred Heart. Claude la Colombière was only the first of Margaret Mary's heart-friends. There had always been an integral connection between the Jesuits and the Visitation. Founder Francis de Sales had been schooled by Jesuits, deeply influenced by their Christian humanist perspective, and formed by the *Spiritual Exercises* that the Society practised. Throughout his life he relied upon Jesuit confessors. Furthermore, from the Order's inception he had recommended to Jane de Chantal that the Jesuit fathers be chosen as confessors for all Visitation monasteries, for he felt these priests alone would understand the unique spirit of the community. Over the decades, the collaboration between Jesuits and Visitandines had continued, even through changing historical circumstances. This was strikingly evident in the city of Paray-le-Monial. By the last quarter of the seventeenth century, the mood of the French Church and society was very different from what it had been at the century's advent. Louis XIV, the Sun King, had risen to ascendancy. To centralise power the king had ended the era of religious tolerance that had existed in

France for almost a century. Huguenots – French Protestants – were expelled and the Roman Church was upheld and militantly promoted. The region in which Paray-le-Monial is located was a region in which wealthy Huguenot families had flourished. After their expulsion, Catholic religious communities such as the Visitation and the Society of Jesus entered the vacuum with missionary fervour to reclaim the populace for the Roman cause. Early modern Catholic Jesuits brought a devotion to the Heart of Christ to their missionary endeavours. So when Claude la Colombière's retreat notes were posthumously published, revealing Margaret Mary's visions, other Jesuit fathers took on the mantle of sponsorship and supported her cause. Two men in particular, Jean Croiset (1656–1738) and Joseph de Gallifet (1663–1749), were active in the effort. The latter was formed under la Colombière's spiritual direction and, as a result of a vow taken when death threatened, dedicated his later years to the promotion of the cult of the Sacred Heart. Gallifet's major work argued the case for the institution of a formal liturgical feast. Jean Croiset's widely circulated book, *The Devotion to the Sacred Heart of Our Lord Jesus Christ*, included a life of Margaret Mary and outlined the motives for practice and cultivation of the Heart devotion.[16] It also contained meditations for various celebrations of the Sacred Heart including the feast in the octave of Corpus Christi, and First Fridays Masses.

The Sacred Heart, with its message of the abundant love of God poured out in Eucharistic streams, was a fitting devotion with which to re-evangelise the land. This process continued into the eighteenth and nineteenth centuries, as the growing influence of the devotion to the Sacred Heart was more and more closely linked to political and social changes in France. While this growth extended far beyond the walls of Visitation cloisters or the pious lay societies the sisters supported, nevertheless the Order remained identified with the Sacred Heart, and at key moments Visitation sisters or monasteries played crucial roles in the devotion's expansion.[17]

The expansion had begun in earnest with Margaret Mary's

unanswered (and perhaps unreceived) vision-induced message for King Louis XIV: the king should engrave the emblem of the Sacred Heart on his standard, his arms, his heart, and the heart of the court. In return for this consecration he was promised victory over his enemies; the king and the Sacred Heart were to be allies in a world divided by heresy and political conflict. This consecration never took place, but the Visitandine's message and the politico-religious hope that it implied did not die with her in 1690. Forty years later, Henri François de Belsunce, Bishop of Marseilles, consecrated his city to the Sacred Heart in the belief that such an action would call down divine favour upon his municipality. The calamity that provoked this public consecration was the arrival of the plague at the port city in 1720. Belsunce was encouraged in his actions by another Visitation nun, Anne-Madeleine Remuzat, from the convent at Marseilles. Like her visionary predecessor, Anne-Madeleine experienced ecstatic union with the Heart of Jesus, participated in an exchange of hearts, engraved the name of Jesus on her breast, and even received the stigmata as a sign of her radical identity with the crucified Lord. Bishop de Belsunce, viewing the plague as a metaphor for the spiritual sickness that French society had contracted, engaged in dramatic public penance for societal sin and consecrated first himself, then later his entire diocese, to the Sacred Heart. The bishop's gestures engaged the Catholic public's imagination: God's wrath could be deflected through religious repentance and supplication; the Catholic community must appeal for relief through the wounded Sacred Heart.

By the end of the eighteenth century the Marseilles story had become a motif in devotional guides intended for public use. It became a spur to the retreating Catholic and royalist forces that battled the formidable momentum of the French Revolution. That violent political upheaval and its long, bloody aftermath profoundly influenced the destiny of the Heart symbol. Although reform factions did not originally intend to attack the church, (a financial crisis of the monarchy was the initiating impulse for the Revolution), events led to a vicious

civil struggle between two transcendent values: the Roman
Catholic God defended by the monarchy and royalist factions,
and the French idea of the Republic. Martyrs fell on both sides.
In the midst of the fray, word of new visions emanating from
an anonymous Visitandine in Nantes circulated. The command
from the suffering Saviour through her was emphatic: revive
the wavering faith of the French people through devotion to
the Sacred Heart.

Mass production of Sacred Heart images began. Convents
across France distributed them as safeguards against harm
and what loyalists saw as the sacrilegious evil of the Revolution. Miracle stories of divine protection abounded. In dozens
of spontaneous ways, the Sacred Heart and its attendant
devotional practices appeared in response to the national
crisis. One fascinating example is recorded in a lengthy letter
penned in 1794 by Mother Marie-Jéronyme Vérot, superior of
the Visitation convent at Lyons.[18] The letter chronicles the fate
of that threatened, and finally disbanded, community as its
members fled the country and reconstituted themselves in
Mantua, Italy. Central to the convent's morale under siege was
the practice of First Friday devotion to the Sacred Heart as it
had been outlined by Margaret Mary. The sisters were also
consoled by having with them (at great risk) the heart of their
founder, Francis de Sales, a relic that they believed bestowed
patronal protection.

Equally representative of the intense identification with the
Heart of Christ among Visitation communities is a prayer from
an eighteenth-century chronicle of the monastery at Nantes.

> Oh, very adorable and most lovable Heart of Jesus, temple
> of the most holy and adorable Trinity, furnace of love,
> ocean of bounty, closet of delights, inexhaustible fountain
> of all graces, it is from You that we wish to imbibe the
> waters of true contrition for not having loved You enough
> and for any offense. Moreover, we choose You for our
> refuge, our asylum, and all our hope. All in general and
> each in particular, we take You for our powerful reformer.

Oh my divine Savior, give us humble hearts, docile to Your grace, contrite, and humble: we pray You by the excess of Your divine mercy. Enclose us in Your divine Heart and hold us there safe against the rage of our enemies visible and invisible, and deliver us from our pride and our self-love and give us hearts truly charitable, so that at last we may begin under the protection of Your divine Heart a cycle of fervor, humility, and precision in all our holy observance. We beg You this grace, O divine Jesus, for the love of Your Sacred Heart, by that of Your holy Mother, of our holy founders, that You may always find among the nuns of our monastery true worshipers, victims, and slaves prepared to obey You. It is to obtain this favor that we offer You a dozen greetings a year and put ourselves in this paper that we have all signed under the feet of the sun (monstrance) where You are enclosed in the adorable Eucharist, having the intention [in] all our communions to renew this same prayer and make honorable amends to Your divine Heart for ourselves and all sinners. Praised and adored be the Heart of Jesus in the Holy Sacrament of the altar. Amen.[19]

The Sacred Heart became the most identifiable emblem of the Counter-revolution. The emergent Republic was characterised as a conspiracy formed against altar and throne, and the Sacred Heart as France's salvation and shield. Part of the popularity of the devotion stemmed from the widely held conviction that King Louis XVI and his household and France itself had been secretly consecrated to the Sacred Heart. Nor did the symbol lose its efficacy after the unfortunate king and his queen were put to death. Indeed, it was the standard under which a series of rebellions were staged as well as the insignia of the ultra-royalist groups that supported the eventual restoration of the monarchy. It was the focal symbol of myriad attempts to re-christianise France in the wake of the compromised Revolution. It was also the chosen emblem of numerous new religious orders that sprang up on the scorched soil.

The distinctive image appeared on the lapels of young Frenchmen who answered the 1860 call to defend the Pope and the papal states against encroaching Italian nationhood. Eventually, the impulse towards national consecration took form in plans to construct a grand church dedicated to the Sacred Heart. The Basilique du Sacré Coeur on Montmartre was originally planned as the Church of the National Vow, a symbol of the marriage of monarchy and Church and the Catholic counter-culture's long fought resistance to the realisation of the aims of revolutionary and republican France.

Eventually, the image of the Sacred Heart spilled out beyond France's borders and its specific preoccupations and became one of the most ubiquitous and defining of Catholic images worldwide. The pattern of devotional observance imagined by Margaret Mary at the close of the seventeenth century was institutionalised in the mid eighteenth as a universal devotion. The Feast was instituted in the liturgical calendar on the Friday following the celebration of Corpus Christi (the Body and Blood of Christ) just as she had requested. Clearly, by this time such a widespread Catholic practice contained overtones of meaning that went well beyond its Salesian beginnings and the world of hearts imagined by Francis de Sales and Jane de Chantal. By the time the obscure Visitandine from Paray was canonised in 1864 by Pope Pius IX, dozens of congregations of religious had been established under its aegis. When Pope Leo XIII consecrated the entire human race to the Sacred Heart in the year 1899, the implication was that this Heart-standard flown over the Church opposed the secularism, scientism, and rationalism of the modern world.

Despite this, the deep grammar of the Margaret Mary-inspired Sacred Heart devotion remained utterly Salesian. It was heart-to-Heart with her beloved Lord, in imitation (and on the Feast day) of John the Beloved Disciple, that the Visitandine received the first of her great revelations. Her intimacy led to an exchange of hearts and the conferral of a new identity – 'Apostle of the Sacred Heart'. The Visitandine motto 'Live Jesus!' became a mission to lead all to the fountain of his

Eucharistic heart. Heart to heart, Margaret Mary and her Jesuit confrères commenced their ministry. And heart to heart – with other Visitandines, laypersons and religious – she communicated her message. The invitation that had been extended to this young Visitandine from the monastery of Paray-le-Monial became an invitation extended to all: 'Behold this Heart which so loves humankind.'

6. THE NINETEENTH-CENTURY SALESIAN PENTECOST

Love is like Jacob's Ladder in that it raises us up to unite our spirit with God and it brings us back again to loving association with our neighbors . . . who are God's image and likeness, created to communicate with the divine goodness, to participate in His grace, and enjoy His glory.[1]

Francis de Sales

Through various channels the Salesian tradition carried its vision of a world of divine and human hearts into the nineteenth century. The lives of founders Francis de Sales and Jane de Chantal continued to be regarded as exemplary. Francis had been canonised in 1665 and Jane in 1767, thus raising them to the status of those models of the Christian life whose feasts are celebrated on the universal Church calendar.[2] In 1877 Francis would be named a Doctor of the Church, a title reserved for those writers whose words are deemed expressive of the fullness of Catholic teaching. The liturgical Sacred Heart devotion, with its Visitandine origins and associations, spread throughout the Catholic world. Margaret Mary Alacoque, too, received official recognition: she was beatified in 1864 and would later be canonised in 1920. And the Order of the Visitation, although like many religious groups severely compromised in Europe during the French Revolution, was introduced into the Americas.

The European society and Church of the early nineteenth century was very different from the society and Church that had given birth to the Salesian tradition two centuries previously. A gradual, but not linear nor universal, process of social de-Christianisation was taking place. The French Revolution had divested the Church of property, interrupted the religious education of a generation, decimated the clergy, destroyed religious communities, and created an antagonism between republican egalitarian ideals and the ideals of a besieged Church. The Napoleonic Wars further aggravated the social chaos. In the wake of this upheaval, as the Church rebounded, a new sort of diocesan clergy was reconstituted. Drawn mainly from the artisan and peasant classes rather than from the upper classes, the new priests generally valued piety over intellectual inquiry and were not as hostile as their predecessors to the popular religion of the time. The clergy were supported by a growing corps of new religious communities, many of them women's communities, formed with the express purpose of educational and healthcare ministry. By mid century these priests and religious had effected a revival of Catholic influence. However, other competing influences – scientism, positivism, and anti-clericalism – increasingly vied for the citizenry's loyalty. Further, the fickle policies of changing political regimes towards the Church contributed to the social turbulence. These trends, seen most clearly in France, were felt as well in neighbouring lands.

The spirituality that emerged by the second half of the nineteenth century retained a certain likeness to the stern Tridentine Catholicism of the eighteenth century.[3] It was still strongly hierarchical and clerically dominated, viewed the world in general and the body in particular as sources of evil, and concentrated on salvation in another world. But a great deal had changed. In particular, the pastoral emphasis on fear and the attempt to impose a rigidly ascetic ideal faded away. The rigorist moral theology of the eighteenth century was softened, and penitential practice turned in a more paternal rather than a juridical direction. Increasingly, pastoral emphasis was put upon the love and forgiveness of God. The reciprocity of divine–human love was seen particularly in the Eucharist. Pilgrimages increased, and a bewildering variety of devotional practices flourished.⁴ It was a world in which the Salesian reign of hearts might easily take hold.

The *Introduction to the Devout Life* continued to be translated and reprinted, entering the ranks of Christian devotional classics. Francis de Sales' other great writing, the *Treatise on the Love of God*, also enjoyed a reputation, even becoming the backbone of priestly formation in some seminaries. As an example of this, in the mid eighteenth century the young Neopolitan Alphonsus Liguori, future founder of the Redemptorist Order, was formed in the Congregation of the Apostolic Missions where Eucharistic piety, Marian devotion and the writings of Francis de Sales were featured. So deep was his Salesian formation that when Liguori took up his pen in later life, he frequently quoted Francis de Sales' words verbatim or liberally used anecdotes from the life of the saintly bishop to illustrate his points. During the nineteenth century, Liguori's moral theology became accepted for use in seminaries across the Catholic world, carrying with it the very Salesian themes of the love of God, conformity to the will of God, confidence in divine mercy and the idea that sanctity is compatible with any state in life, as well as a deeply Salesian sense of gentleness and the art of winning hearts in pastoral care.⁵ Liguori, of course, brought his own nuances to the task, shaped as he was by the religious climate of his era.⁶

But Salesian spirituality was not only carried in its early institutions and literary expressions, or filtered through the lens of others' work. In the mid nineteenth century the tradition came newly to life in fresh expressions, mainly through the foundation of religious communities and secular societies placed under the patronage of St Francis de Sales and dedicated to spreading the Salesian spiritual vision. This phenomenon has been termed the 'Salesian Pentecost' by Salesian scholar Henri l'Honoré.⁷ The present discussion does not exhaust the list of varying groups that were imprinted to greater or lesser degrees with the Salesian spirit, but it highlights those significant foundations that are genuine, while distinctive, expressions of the Salesian world of hearts.⁸

APOSTLES OF THE CHABLAIS: THE MISSIONARIES FROM ANNECY

To love God with one's whole heart, soul and strength, and one's neighbour like oneself, this is the unique necess[ity], this is the missionary, this is the apostle, this is happiness.[9]

Pierre-Joseph Mermier

Annecy, 'dear Nessy' as Francis and Jane had called it, had been his episcopal see. The Visitation had been born there in the little 'Gallery House' just across the town from the bishop's cathedral that overlooked the alpine lake that bore the city's name. By the year 1830, the Savoyard region, as with so many regions in Europe, was recovering from the trauma inflicted by the French Revolution and its aftermath. Eight years earlier, the diocese of Annecy had been re-established, having been suppressed during the years of revolutionary conflict. With re-establishment came the need to evangelise the population, an entire generation of whom were uncatechised.

In 1838, with the prompting and approval of Pierre Joseph Rey, Bishop of Annecy (1770–1842), Father Pierre-Marie Mermier (1790–1862) and five other diocesan priests covenanted to live in community under a rule permeated with the Salesian spirit. St Francis de Sales was their patron and the model for their lives of apostolic, missionary zeal. Thus was born the Congregation of the Missionaries of St Francis de Sales of Annecy. In fact, the little band of men had already been engaged in giving parish missions to re-evangelise Savoy before 1838. But with the formation of the new community, the Salesian aegis was formally raised over the group. Their rule required that members engage in continuous study of the works of St Francis and follow both his spirit and his method of preaching and apostolic work.[10]

Both Bishop Rey and Father Mermier had suffered under the religious suppression and, both, as they once again tasted religious freedom, were eager to re-evangelise their native lands. Both felt that the mantle of St Francis de Sales, who in his own day had engaged in re-evangelisation, had fallen upon them. Rey was in fact born in the Chablais, the very region Francis had helped reclaim for the Catholic faith. Rey had studied both in Thonon, the town in which Francis' mission had its headquarters, and at the seminary in Francis' beloved Annecy. During the Terror Rey had made the mountains of Savoy the site of his clandestine priestly activity. When the Diocese of Annecy was re-established he became, like his lauded predecessor, its chief shepherd. Mermier too had faced the brutal reality of the Terror. His boyhood family farm between Annecy and Geneva was the site of many a secret midnight Mass said by priests fleeing the republican police. After his ordination to the priesthood, Mermier had joined forces with Father Joseph Marie Favre to stir up religious fervour in their village parish. Soon, the two embarked on a mission to preach in Savoy with Mermier focusing on Annecy and Favre on Chambéry. An early dream of combining forces and uniting under the name 'Oblates of St Francis de Sales' never materialised, but eventually, after a stint as spiritual director of the Annecy seminary, Mermier with several companions formed a community at the town of La Roche. The Rule that emerged out of the La Roche beginnings was chiefly crafted from the Rule of the Vincentians which, in its turn, made extensive use of the *Directory of the Visitation* written by Francis de Sales. Then, with the support of Bishop Rey, the nascent community moved into a newly built house near the seminary. Over the main altar was placed a statue of St Francis de Sales.

Bishop Rey further advanced the cause of the missionary priests when he bequeathed to them the property of Les Allinges, including the historic chapel in which, during his own missionary forays, de Sales had often celebrated Mass. It was Rey who sponsored the restoration of the site and who promoted pilgrimages there.

. . . the missionaries will consider Les Allinges as the

headquarters where the souvenir of their model and patron will be [seen] vividly everywhere and will enkindle fervour in their noble and holy work of the missions.[11]

The year 1838 was thus both the culmination of many years' work and the beginning of a new venture under the express patronage of the Salesian founder.

The patron and special protector of the Congregation is St Francis de Sales, as the faithful imitator of Jesus Christ and all his virtues, particularly His love for sinners and His meekness [gentleness] which he practiced with such heroism. With the grace of God and the intercession of this Blessed Patron, the missionaries named after him will profess to imitate these virtues in a special manner. (Constitutions of 1838)[12]

Mermier's apostolic spirit never abated. When he saw a need, he addressed it. What he saw was that educational opportunities for young girls of poorer classes were few. Furthermore, many poor unmarried girls from the countryside had insufficient dowries to enter religious communities. With the co-operation of Claudine Echernier, housekeeper for a parish priest who had developed an *ad hoc* school for girls in the kitchen of the rectory at a small parish in Chavanod, Mermier, her spiritual guide, founded a cognate women's community under Salesian patronage.[13] The innovative rule of the Congregation of the Daughters of the Holy Cross established two categories of sisters: those who lived with their parents or masters and did manual work and those who lived in community as sister-teachers or sister-workers. In keeping with the spirit of the early Visitation with its unique entrance requirements, the Holy Cross nuns were to accept the poor, untutored, and elderly if they had a true call.[14] The women were to work mainly among the poor of the countryside.

Thus the legacy of preaching heart to heart, of gentle persuasion yoked to pastoral zeal, the universal call to holiness, and the vision of a world of hearts fuelled by the fires of love came to life again in nineteenth-century Savoy. Interestingly, what began in the Missionaries of Annecy as an internal effort to re-Catholicise Europe soon became an order that evangelised chiefly in foreign territory. In 1845 the Portuguese colonial territory in India with the vicarate of Vizag was entrusted to the care of the Missionaries of Annecy. It was there that the order prospered under a succession of devout leaders and, in the twenty-first century, has its chief ministry, although the community has also made foundations in places as diverse as Germany, Brazil, England and Algeria.[15]

Mermier, as superior of an expanding community, continually steeped himself in daily meditation on the works of his patron and recommended the same programme to his missionaries. As a result, many of the sayings that survive in his letters reveal his instinctive grasp of Salesian principles, especially the practice of the little virtues and living between the two wills of God.

On the Rule:

> To Fr Thevenet in India: Self-denial, readiness to accept discomfort, to be all to all, everywhere, in the least things, like the grain of wheat buried in the ground. Charity and kindness to one's neighbour are the daughters of God's love.

To missionaries going to India:

> Be cheerful and helpful, yet preserving modesty and a certain reserve, bear willingly with the defects of your fellow travelers ... At the Customs, dealing with Officials, dealing with anyone, be always honest, be good to everyone, never causing trouble to anyone ...

To his niece, Sr Louise Mermier:

> Don't refuse any office, any kind of work, however vile or disgusting it may appear in itself. Obedience, love of God, turn everything into gold.

To Fr Delalex, India:

We do much when we do little, if we do it for God, when
and as He wants it.

To Fr F. Decompoix, India:

What the Lord wants of us is this: uprightness, purity of
intention, faithfulness in our work, not the quantity, but
the quality.

To Fr Tissot, the future Bishop of Vizag:

. . . Beware of the poison of vainglory, work for a greater
simplicity, purify your intentions, yes, in the manner of St
Francis de Sales. It's just what the Common Rule pre-
scribes, 'Each one will have the purest intention of
pleasing God alone.' 'Pray for your superior, that he may
begin to practice, though so late, what he preaches to his
masters . . .'[16]

At the centre of the missionary endeavour, no matter where,
was the parish mission. The Salesian legacy of preaching heart
to heart and thus drawing listeners closer to God was one that
the new community fostered. Like their predecessor during
his sojourn in the Chablais, the Missionaries of Annecy made
full use of the devotional and liturgical repertoire of the Roman
Catholic tradition to stir hearts. Francis himself had reintroduced the Forty Hours Devotion to the Eucharist at Thonon.
His spiritual sons went even further, developing a richly tex-
tured pattern for the parish mission that involved the whole
community and engaged the participants body, mind and heart.

As the missionaries entered a village, church bells were
rung, the townspeople gathered, and a procession to the church
culminated in a welcome from the parish priest. Next day, a
festive high Mass took place; music, prayers and an invitation
to participate in the coming 15 to 21 days went out. During
the course of the mission, daily exercises, at 5:30 a.m., 9 a.m.
and 3 p.m., were held in the church. These could include catechetical instruction, sermons on truths of the faith and
Christian living, benediction of the sacrament, examination of

conscience, hymns, instructions on prayer and explanation of the commandments. Sermons were always done in the Salesian manner, simply and directed towards moving hearts and thus changing lives for the greater love of God. Then there were celebrations scattered throughout the next fortnight that included para-liturgical ceremonies with candles and flowers, and tableaux of biblical scenes. There were celebrations for children, for the dead, and for various feasts, especially those associated with the Virgin Mary. In addition, the missionaries, usually in pairs, held 'dialogue conferences' on religious topics. One priest would represent the 'Devil's Advocate', the other, from the pulpit, would explain Catholic truth. The dialogues were laced with humour and lively stories and attracted large crowds. The Missionaries always made themselves available for confession and often had penitents return three or four times to encourage them to truly amend their lives. This concern for lasting effectiveness led the community to begin sponsoring local confraternities (faith support groups) organised by gender or marital status. These spiritual cells would continue to nurture the heart-stirrings that the parish mission had evoked long after the Missionaries had moved on.

Thus the vision of the world of hearts, transformed through preaching, teaching and ministry, that lodged so deep in Francis de Sales' own heart, was brought to life after his death in the very region where two centuries previously he had preached heart to heart.

'PREVENTIVE PEDAGOGY': THE FAMILY OF DON BOSCO SALESIANS[17]

This oratory is placed under this patronage of St Francis de Sales, because those who intend to dedicate themselves to this kind of work should adopt this saint as a model of charity and affability. These sources will produce the fruits that we expect from the Oratories.[18]

Don Bosco

Ordinary Catholics had for centuries held the 'holy protectors' of their local towns, trades and parishes in high regard. These heavenly patrons were called upon to combat evil and further the interests of those who prayed to them. Popular piety in the nineteenth-century northern Italian peninsula was no different. St Francis de Sales, while never regarded as a great popular wonderworker, was nevertheless a son of Savoy. And so it made sense that he should have been remembered and claimed as a favourite son in Turin and the surrounding region of the Piedmont.[19] It was especially among the educated classes of Catholics that the memory of de Sales was vividly alive there in the nineteenth century, although it would be a Piedmontese man born of peasant stock who would so internalise the Salesian world of hearts that from a vision for the élite, the heart to heart spirit would become the inheritance of the poorest and most marginalised populations in Turin and, eventually, throughout the world.

Religious practice in Savoy, as in France, had been deeply disrupted by the French Revolution and the Napoleonic Wars. In the renewal that followed, the heart-centred vision of the 'apostle of the Chablais' was promoted. The regions around Annecy, the Chablais and the Piedmont had long been yoked together under the leadership of the royal house of Savoy. At the royal court, a distinctive high culture had been cultivated. And at the core of the region's ancient cultural identity was the Roman Catholic faith. In Turin, at the *Convitto Ecclesiastico*, a training ground for clerical renewal, Francis de Sales was presented to parish priests destined for rural service as a model for the pastoral care of souls. His works, along with the writings of Alphonsus Liguori, were read and editions of his spiritual maxims were circulated. It was especially Joseph Cafasso (1811–1860), a dedicated instructor at the *Convitto* as well as an inspired preacher and spiritual guide, known as the 'pearl of the Italian clergy', who promoted the bishop-saint for emulation. When Cafasso sent his charges out to work among the unchurched of the city, he held up de Sales.

Give me souls, O Lord. Let us say [these words] with that great apostolic charity of St Francis de Sales. Give me souls to save! Give me sins to combat, to exterminate. Let us leave those who want the madness and pomp of this world to have all they want, while we apply our efforts to increase the population of paradise.[20]

Among Cafasso's disciples was a remarkable young priest, who had risen from the peasantry, John Bosco (1815–1888). John hailed from Becchi, a hamlet of Castelnuovo d'Asti in the Piedmont, and from an early age had dreamed of becoming a priest. His dream was not easily realised as his widowed mother relied upon his help to survive. Nevertheless, John persisted, and his gifts and tenacity eventually brought him to the doorway of the *Convitto* for a three-year programme in pastoral formation and into Cafasso's orbit, within which the young man was imbued with the Salesian spirit. John had not, however, come to the seminary ignorant of the bishop-saint on whom he would model his own priestly career. The city of Chieri, where Bosco received his first formal schooling, boasted an active system of lay confraternities, one of which was under the patronage of St Francis. More significantly, the diocesan seminary in the town, where John studied from 1835 to 1841, claimed both Sts Francis de Sales and Philip Neri as patrons. The feast days of these two were lavishly celebrated and their examples very much alive. As he composed his resolutions on the eve of his ordination to the priesthood, John Bosco wrote, 'May the charity and sweetness of St Francis de Sales guide me in everything.'[21]

Further, early in his priestly career, John had been employed as a chaplain at the *Rifugio*, a 'house of refuge' in Turin for country girls escaping from prostitution. The *Rifugio* was one of several charitable initiatives sponsored by the Marchesa Barolo, a pious and indefatigable benefactor of the city's poor. One of the Marchesa's plans, never realised, was to establish a corps of priests to serve her many charities. She envisioned the group being put under the protection of St Francis. In fact, the women's congregation that did emerge from the *Rifugio* was clearly shaped by Salesian principles.[22] It was while he was under the employ of Marchesa Barolo that John Bosco gathered a small group of working-class youngsters for religious instruction on Sundays and holidays in two rooms the Marchesa owned.

> ... [T]hat charitable lady was happy to put at our disposal for use as a chapel two large rooms intended for the recreation of the priests of the Refuge when they should transfer their residence there ... that was the site Divine Providence chose for the first Oratory church. We began to call it after St Francis de Sales ... because Marchesa Barolo had in mind to found a congregation of priests under his patronage and with this intention she had a painting of this saint done, which can still be seen at the entrance to this area.[23]

It was later, under Cafasso's tutelage at the *Convitto*, that Bosco's deep appreciation and embrace of Francis de Sales as model and guide, hinted at before, crystallised; and the work that would occupy him for the rest of his life began.

The Festive Oratory of St Francis de Sales

The plight of working-class youngsters was never far from John's mind. His own modest beginnings gave him an empathy and instinct for common folk. Early in his priestly career he formed friendships with street children and, concerned that they had no one to care for them, he created what he called his Festive Oratory of St Francis de Sales. In his *Memoirs of the Oratory*, Bosco often makes note of the prophetic dreams that guided him into the future. A boyhood dream at the age of nine seems to have revealed his future ministry and to have instructed him. He saw a crowd of cursing, fighting boys and heard the instruction, 'You will have to win these friends of yours, not with blows but with gentleness and kindness. So begin right now to show them that sin is ugly and virtue beautiful.'[24] The sensitivity foreshadowed in this dream stayed with John all his life. Not only was he concerned for the material needs of poor youth, but he perceived the essential human goodness discovered beneath often tough, hardened exteriors. (In his dream the boys, whose behaviour scandalised pious John, were designated his 'friends'.) This was an eminently Salesian perspective and it made it possible for the future priest to communicate heart to heart. The Festive Oratory of his creation would be an environment where these children of God, who came in the trappings of tough, impoverished, often abused boys, could begin to realise their true dignity. The saint from Savoy taught John how.

> We had put our own ministry, which called for great calm and meekness, under the protection of this saint in the hope that he might obtain for us from God the grace of being able to imitate him in his extraordinary meekness and in winning souls.[25]

Like Francis before him, Bosco was gentle and approachable. And, like his model, he had unflagging zeal. In his desire to win the hearts of these neglected boys, he encountered much opposition. Not from the boys, who flocked to him, but from respectable folks who did not want hordes of disreputable youths gathering in their neighbourhoods. Eventually, John was able to acquire property in Turin's Valdocco neighbourhood and to build a church to accommodate the growing number of youngsters who came to him. A contemporary observer made note of the new foundations.

> In these two houses, Turin's true wretches [*cendiosi*] and true scamps [*biricchini*] come together on feast days in great numbers. It is amazing to see how much they love it, how happy they are, and how well they behave while there. We see match vendors, lottery ticket vendors, etc., etc., apprentices, work hands, houseboys, youngsters from all kinds of workshops and trades, all happy together. And what precisely do all these young people do in these new

houses of shelter? In the first place, they are given some
religious instruction by those zealous priests [. . . then
they pray, they have classes, they play, and occasionally
they get a snack in the afternoon].[26]

Yoking respectful caring, education, advocacy, devotion, and
popular piety together in a spirit of joyful play, Bosco's programmes inculcated the boys with a sense of self-worth and
responsibility. Intellectual training went hand in hand with
celebration, and there were many festivals to celebrate during
the church year. The feast of the holy patron, Francis de Sales,
was observed in a more subdued way than most: as an oppor-
tunity for ongoing formation during which the week-long
'conference of Saint Francis de Sales' encouraged Christian
virtue.

John Bosco's methods of formation were practical and grew
out of an instinctive sense of what worked. When boys first
came to him, he drew them heart to heart by games and
walks into the country, coupled with religious instruction. The
gentleness he so admired in de Sales' character was always
evident in his own. Appreciation and encouragement rather
than punishment were his methods. Love rather than fear was
the motive for improvement, and it seems to have worked.
Often called the 'preventive system' this flexible and innovative approach to winning hearts was remarkable for its
effectiveness. In Don Bosco's own words,

> The young constitute the most fragile yet most valuable
> component of human society, for we base our hopes for the
> future on them. They are not of themselves depraved.
> Were it not for parental neglect, idleness, mixing in bad
> company, something they experience especially on
> Sundays and holy days, it would be so easy to inculcate
> in their young hearts moral and religious principles – of
> order, good behavior, respect, religious practice. For if they
> are found to have been ruined at that young age, it will
> have been due more to thoughtlessness than to ingrained
> malice. These young people have real need of some kind

person who will care for them, work with them, guide them in virtue, keep them away from evil... Oratories should be reckoned among the most effective means for instilling the religious spirit into the uncultivated hearts of neglected young people.[27]

The Salesian Family

The history of the Oratory is a study in invention and calls to mind the phrase often associated with Francis de Sales' contemporary and friend, Vincent de Paul, who was also influenced by the vision of a world of hearts: 'inventive to infinity'. John Bosco wanted to win hearts, and he used any means to do so. His spiritual posture, however, was unchanging: gentle persuasion linked to pastoral zeal. When support for the Oratory waned, he enlisted his own mother, who came to live among the boys her son tended. When the illiteracy of his charges weighed on him, he opened a night school to provide education for youngsters who worked during the day. When lack of a skill forced his boys to live off the streets, he organised artisan-training programmes. When the helpers he had enlisted were not adequate to the task, he began his own communities. In 1848 his first seminarian donned the cassock and came to live at the Oratory, marking the first step towards the creation of a congregation of men dedicated to Bosco's ministries and formed in the Salesian method. The community would receive official recognition in 1859 and definitive papal approval in 1874. They would be known as the Salesians after St Francis de Sales who served as their double model of gentle loving-kindness and apostolic urgency.

Among Bosco's first followers was Michael Rua, who would become one of the first Salesians as well as Don Bosco's successor as superior of the vast Salesian family. Rua's story exemplifies the way the Salesian family grew. Eight-year-old Michael first came to the Festive Oratory at the invitation of a friend. Although his family was struggling, the boy's mother had misgivings about her youngest child associating with the rough children who frequented the Oratory. But Bosco saw in him a gift and a call. The elder man encouraged the boy to study Latin and put him in charge of students walking home from Oratory-sponsored events. Eventually Rua prepared for and entered the priesthood. He was entrusted with weekly catechism classes, then put in charge of the library, then made responsible for the satellite Oratories that were springing up. Increasing responsibilities followed: finally Rua became major superior of the congregation following Bosco's death in 1888 (an event which shook the younger man to the core) and succeeded in preserving and expanding the work that his mentor had begun. An echo of Visitation spirituality can be heard in the often-repeated characterisation of Rua: he was 'the living Rule'.

The men's congregation, Salesians of Don Bosco, emerged from practical necessity. But the founder had never imagined the Christian life as primarily clerical or male in character. In fact, his first associates were all laypeople, women as well as men, who were inspired by his vision of Christian perfection practised precisely through active service to the most marginalised. Canon law of the time could not accommodate a religious community composed of laity and clerics or of women and men. So Bosco created cognate societies parallel to his men's religious community: for laypeople, the Union of Salesian Co-operators (1875),[28] and for women religious, the Daughters of Mary Help of Christians. In the *Treatise on the Love of God* Francis de Sales had written eloquently of the two aspects of love, affective and effective, that were realised in love of God and love of one's neighbour. He had written equally eloquently of the call of all people, lay and cleric, women and men, to embrace the fullness of love. In the nineteenth century this vision was concretised in the Piedmont in the Salesian spiritual family.

It is necessary for Christians to unite in the doing of good works . . . We Christians ought to be united in these difficult times to promote the spirit of prayer, of charity

with all the means that religion furnishes and so remove
or at least mitigate those evils which jeopardize the good
morals of growing youth in whose hands rests the destiny
of civil society.[29]

Daughters of Mary Help of Christians

Canonical restrictions had not only made it difficult to create
a society in which laypeople and clerics could work side by
side, it was also difficult for John to establish a community of
women religious to serve his rapidly expanding ministries.
There was some canonical precedent for his flexible community
of men dedicated to active apostolic work. The Salesians had
grown quickly; by the time of Bosco's death in 1888, there
would be 250 community houses in all parts of the world
serving 130,000 children, and more than 6,000 priests would
be formed in his institutions, over 1,200 of whom would remain
within Salesian ministries. But the Church was not as flexible
in its views governing women's communities, especially those
engaged in apostolic work. Nevertheless, the social need was
great and need gave rise to invention. At the same time that
traditional contemplative orders were being suppressed by
civil government, new, creative women's institutes were
springing up everywhere to respond to pressing social issues
of the poor and uneducated. Between 1815 and 1846, 183 new
female foundations were approved by the Church; 104 of these
were in northern Italy.[30] These communities were active in
orientation and, to conform to canonical norms, were organised
as 'third orders' associated with or aggregated to men's orders.
This was the model that Bosco would employ.

The Piedmontese priest had long been aware that his successful ministries for young men did not reach their sisters.
To redress this reality, he had often collaborated with existing
women's groups or with women like Benedetto Savio, a devout
woman living as *la monaca en casa* (a nun at home)[31] in his
home town, or with Marie-Louise Clarac, a Sister of Charity
who built a daycare centre, a clinic, and an elementary school

for poor girls in Turin. All of Bosco's collaborators were engaged in one way or another with the education and formation of children at risk. But it was Maria Domenica Mazzarello (1837–1881) who would formally work with Bosco to create a women's institute in the Salesian family to meet the needs of society's most neglected girls.[32]

The Piedmontese priest and this woman from the Mornese first met in the autumn of 1864 when he came to her town. On that occasion they did not meet in private but Maria participated with the other townspeople in the celebrations occasioned by the visit of the youth worker from Turin. Later John conversed with the parish women's sodality that served women in need and of which Maria was a member. This pious association, the Daughters of Mary Immaculate, had been introduced to the parish by the same priest who served as Maria's spiritual guide. This priest, in his turn, had received the idea for the association from Don Frassinetti, a Genoese prelate formed in the spiritual tradition of Alphonsus Liguori, a tradition that actively promoted small faith-based groups to renew the life of the church. The vision of Christian perfection that John Bosco laid out before the parish group in the Mornese – the beauty of virtue, the duty to give a good example, the vision of life lived in love and service of God – inflamed young Maria's imagination.

When the Daughters of Mary split into two groups, with one taking private vows as nuns at home, a second gathered around Maria and moved into a common dwelling where they prayed together and taught home-making skills to needy town girls. When Don Bosco returned to the Mornese in 1868 to consecrate the new church, he took note of the fledgling community. By 1874, his own growing sense that a women's community should be 'aggregated' to the Salesians was confirmed, and the Institute of the Daughters of Mary Help of Christians came into being. Maria Mazzarello and her companions, unlike many of the Salesian priests and brothers who were drawn from among Bosco's abandoned boys, were from pious Catholic peasant families and were already engaged in active service when they joined the Salesian family.

Early in her life, Maria had been drawn to apostolic service as a result of trauma. In her girlhood she had been felled during an epidemic of typhoid fever while caring for ailing relatives and her health had been broken. As a result, she began to reflect upon her life and gradually gave herself in service of others. A workshop to train women as dressmakers was an outworking of that reflection. Deeply moved by Don Bosco's presence – she deemed him a Saint from her first glimpse of him – Maria was drawn naturally into the Salesian family. Her already-mature spirituality enriched the spiritual family she adopted. In her ministry, Maria felt that it was necessary to understand the temperament of each person in order to be supportive and encouraging. In addition, the negative emphasis on sin, hell and the devil, found in some Catholic spiritual writers of the period, was not evident in her pastoral approach. Rather, in true Salesian fashion, Maria stressed the power of trusting heart to heart human relationships in spiritual direction, friendship and family. She possessed a Salesian optimism in the human capacity for God and for spiritual growth. And she advocated a holistic religiosity that honoured work, health, humour and joyful appreciation of life.[33] The Salesian flavour of gentleness and the by-then time-honoured practice of winning hearts, so reminiscent of Jane de Chantal, was always evident in her correspondence to members of her institute as they, with the Salesian Society, expanded their ministry around the globe.

> I regret to hear that things are not going on so well in the new house of Las Piedras [Uruguay, South America]. Sr Giovanna is too young, and is not as yet capable of taking the place of the Superior. However, there is no need to worry, remember, that there will always be defects, we must correct and remedy whatever we can, but always with great calm, leaving everything in the hands of God. However, do not pay too much attention to trifles.

Sometimes in the effort to keep track of so many small things, matters of importance are let pass . . . Correct, warn always, but with great compassion and kindness to all.[34]

The optimism, humanism and compassion so characteristic of Francis de Sales and Jane de Chantal's spirits are evident in the spirit that suffuses the Salesian family brought into being two centuries later by John Bosco. The children entrusted to the spiritual family's care were not only to be loved but were to be told repeatedly, by the Salesians, the Daughters of Mary Help of Christians and the Salesian Co-operators, that they were lovable and loved. In the deeply scriptural imagination of Francis de Sales, love conquered all. From this followed the idea that in all interactions every hint of coercion was to be avoided. In like fashion, Don Bosco's 'preventive method' was anchored in loving – care freed from all physical coercion. For both the Savoyard and the Piedmontese, the love of God was practical and heartfelt. Loving God faithfully consisted in loving those whom one had been given, whatever one's state in life. Little things, insignificant acts even, done with love and pure intent, and for the least, were the royal road to perfection.[35]

Over the centuries, the Salesian family of Don Bosco flowered. In the twenty-first century that spiritual family, which encompasses all of the varied communities that share the lifestyle, pastoral and educational approach and spiritual heritage inspired by John Bosco, has a global presence and includes the third largest Catholic men's order and the second largest Catholic women's community in the world.

THE PARIS CONNECTION: MONSEIGNEUR DE SÉGUR, HENRI CHAUMONT AND THE DAUGHTERS

If other saints, more austere of aspect, cut down the 'false self' with an iron sword, Francis de Sales, smilingly cuts down the same false self with a sword made of sugar. As much as one might want sugar, the old self will be gone for good.[36]

Louis Gaston de Ségur

Always, in the Salesian view, one heart on fire with the love of God can kindle a similar flame in other hearts. In mid nineteenth century Paris, one man's heart was captured by the vision first imagined by Francis de Sales and Jane de Chantal, and out of love for that vision he spent a lifetime kindling the same love in other hearts. Louis Gaston de Ségur was born in the French capital in 1820 and died there in 1881. From that epicentre of French culture, his influence would spread throughout the land. The Ségur name had been a notable one in France for over six centuries: his father and cousin claimed the title of Count, and his uncle was a Chevalier in the royal military order of St Louis. On his mother's side, young Louis claimed a noble Russian lineage. Educated at a variety of institutions, the boy reached the age of eighteen with only a shadow of Christian faith. This state of religious indifference was radically reversed through contact with his Russian grandmother, the Countess Rostopchine, who along with her literary and artistic mentoring, offered Louis Gaston a copy of the *Introduction to the Devout Life*. Making a retreat with de Sales' meditations as a guide, the young man was converted to a life dedicated to God. Like Francis de Sales before him, young Ségur's father had a law career in mind for his son, but the Parisian had his own sights set on the priesthood. Despite family resistance, he entered the seminary of St Sulpice and was ordained in 1847. At the seminary he found that the warm, accessible spirituality of the Salesian founders balanced the austere abnegation taught by the French School.[37] De Sales, along with Francis of Assisi, Charles Borromeo and King Louis, would remain his saintly patrons throughout his life.

Ségur's own conversion experience filled him with the desire to convert the population in the capital, an area notable for its lack of Catholic adherence. Ministry to the poor, young people and imprisoned soldiers occupied the young priest until he was called to Rome to become an auditor for the Rota. While there, he was instrumental in founding a French seminary. In the eternal city he gained the esteem of Pope Pius IX who would become an avid supporter of Ségur's ambitious plans for the defence and preservation of the Catholic faith. Eventually, rapid loss of eyesight brought him back to his native land where he received the honours and privileges of the episcopal office. Although in Paris Ségur would become a prolific writer – of apologetic tracts meant to convince the irreligious and spiritual works aimed to spread Salesian principles in opposition to rigid, Jansenistic traditions – he is most remembered for the various apostolic communities he founded under the patronage of St Francis de Sales.

Louis Gaston's heart had been won to the Salesian world of hearts. He commenced his new sight-impaired life in Paris physically but not spiritually compromised, and on the January feast day of St Francis de Sales, put himself under the tutelage of 'that most holy, indulgent and wise of all spiritual guides, whose doctrine was no less ravishing than his charity and common sense'.[38] Those who, in their turn, came to Ségur for spiritual advice – and they were many – found in him a gentle guide to whom they might open their hearts. A 1879 letter to a young man seeking his counsel illustrates his pastoral sensitivity.

> I care for you with my whole heart; you have good reason to call me your father. You make me feel like a father by having confidence in me and being so vulnerable. I wish that you might also make me feel so by taking seriously the advice I give you.[39]

The Association of Francis de Sales

Ten years after his ordination, Monseigneur de Ségur began preparations for the Salesian works that would occupy him for the remainder of his life. The mature Parisian's pastoral concerns were many, but he became increasingly concerned about the challenges to Catholic life and practice: secularisation, anti-clericalism, and militant Protestant evangelisation. With the support of Pius IX, he gathered together a remarkable group of fervent Catholic leaders from all over France who met in his episcopal salon in 1857. Representatives from the Jesuit, Dominican, Lazarist (Vincentian), Oratorian and Sulpician orders, with diocesan priests including Gaspard Mermillod from Savoy (future successor of de Sales to the See of Geneva) and Louis Brisson from the diocese of Troyes, were present. Both of these latter prelates were to be prime movers in the promotion of Salesian spirituality, especially Mermillod who, as Cardinal, would urge Francis' teachings in a variety of settings.[40] An association whose articulated goal was the defence and promotion of the Catholic faith was formed. Ségur became its president. The Savoyard 'Apostle of the Chablais' was chosen as patron. Thus was born the Association of St Francis de Sales. Paris was to be the centre – the heart – out from which the fires of charity would radiate. Diocesan directors and sub-directors were appointed to facilitate the spread of the flames. But, in typically Salesian fashion, there was to be no authoritarian chain of command. Rather, the Association in each diocese was to adapt its goals and projects in response to the local situation. Ségur would play the part of inspirer and encourager. Over the years he would found several institutes himself and he would serve as long-distance supporter of many others in dioceses all over Europe. When he visited local chapters he preached the love of God heart to heart and left all direction up to local leadership. By the year 1881 the Association numbered 1,900,000 members.[41]

Monseigneur de Ségur's own diocese benefited from several specific initiatives. One year after the inaugural meeting in his Paris salon, the bishop organised a group of his own priests which he named the Priests of St Francis de Sales. Their association existed for the mutual sanctification of its members and the evangelisation of the environs of Paris. His priests lent their services to the overburdened parish clergy by preaching, leading missions and retreats and providing catechetical instruction for parishioners. A typical mission might yield scores of baptisms, regularised marriages, confirmations and first communions. The successful model spread to other dioceses. Much to its founder's regret, administration of the society of priests was eventually delegated to local leadership, and, after many vibrant years, the apostolate ceased to exist. A campaign to increase respect for the Sunday sabbath in the French capital also had a brief life.

While he was nurturing others in the Salesian spirit, Monseigneur de Ségur was being nurtured by the Visitandine expression of that same spirit. He was a frequent visitor at the monastery on rue de Vaugirard where his sister Sabine was a member, and he formed a deep spiritual friendship with another sister, Marie-Donat Poisson, who cared for Sabine in her last illness. Sr Marie-Donat was several years his senior and fabled for her simplicity. Ségur maintained an affectionate correspondence with her for many years.[42] Expressive of the bond between this great patron of the Salesian Pentecost and the Visitation is the fact that after their deaths both his and his mother's hearts were preserved in reliquaries and honoured at the convent on rue de Vaugirard.[43] Moreover, during his extensive travels, the Paris dignitary always paid a visit to the Visitation communities in the cities where the Association was promoted. He was especially fond of the communities at Annecy and at Troyes where the remarkable superior, Marie de Sales Chappuis, who had for a time been a superior in Paris, promoted the Association with special vigour.

Despite the fact that the Visitation Order had suffered setbacks during the political upheavals occasioned by the Revolution and its long aftermath, the Order still played a prominent role in the resurgent Catholic world. The promotion of the Sacred Heart devotion is a case in point. Another example of this, far from Paris but perhaps more familiar to modern readers, is the case of Thérèse of Lisieux, the Carmelite saint whose 'Little Way' has had such currency in the years since her death in 1897.[44] Thérèse Martin grew up in an intensely pious atmosphere liberally tinged with Salesian influence. As her sister Léonie, a Vistandine of Caen, would write during her interview for the process of Thérèse's 1910 beatification, '. . . there is a great devotion to her in all our convents. This is not surprising, however, because her piety is the same spirit as ours and as that of our holy founder, Francis de Sales.'[45]

All over the continent, similar stories of the continuing Salesian influence through the Visitation could be recounted.

Henri Chaumont, Caroline Carré de Malberg and the Daughters of Francis de Sales

As early as 1850, Ségur had become aware of a young man destined to become a principal in the Salesian Pentecost. Henri Chaumont (1838–1896) was presented to the elder man on the eve of his first communion at St Sulpice. Ségur prophetically noted to the boy's mother that her son seemed destined for the priesthood.[45] Such was in fact the case and nine years later Chaumont found himself at the seminary in Issy. Mealtime reading of Francis de Sales' letters in the refectory caught the seminarian's interest and he began a study of the Savoyard's teachings which would continue for the remainder of his life. That passion was further encouraged when Ségur arranged for a venerable spiritual director at St Sulpice, Fr Grandvaux, to guide the young man. Encouraging his attraction to Salesian spirituality, Grandvaux also encouraged Chaumont's growing dream of founding an association for people in the world desiring to develop spiritually. These devout people would be formed by principles developed by Francis de Sales. Accordingly, Chaumont began to collate the advice of the Saint, picking out quotations from his many written works and arranging them under the headings of the virtues. These treatises on the virtues from a Salesian perspective would become the centre of the formation programme for those seeking to deepen their spiritual lives.

Chaumont was aware of the initiatives of the Association of

Francis de Sales. Soon he was made vicar of the popular Paris parish of St Marcel and tried to infuse the community with the Salesian spirit by means of faith-formation groups. One of his great hopes was to gather a group of priests formed in the life of Salesian virtue who would, through varied ministries, renew the spiritual lives of the diocesan clergy. He also concerned himself with the spiritual vitality of the Christian household. To that end he sought to form wives and mothers in the vision of a world of hearts. Chaumont was to be most successful in his foundation of a society for laity with the specific end:

> ... To allow lay women, who have a spiritual inclination, to become familiar with the guidelines for a life of perfection proposed by Francis de Sales, and to spread these teachings ... extracted from the *Introduction to the Devout Life*; to stimulate and nurture a spiritual family of those who adopt these guidelines; to create thus a sort of religious institute without vows for those who remain in the world, and not excluding married persons.[47]

This Salesian project had been welcomed and approved by no less than Mother Marie de Sales Chappuis of Troyes and by Genevan Bishop Mermillod whom Chaumont had visited along his pilgrimage route to Annecy. At the Sainte Source the pilgrim had prayed before the Salesian founders' tombs and asked for their intercession on the project's behalf. The dreamt-of apostolate became a reality when Chaumont was transferred to Ste-Clothilde parish where he came into contact with Madame Carré de Malberg, a former student at the Visitation at Metz and wife of Commandant Paul Carré. Deeply religious, intelligent and energetic, Caroline Carré de Malberg revealed her spiritual depths as she struggled with the successive deaths of her four children. When she arrived in Paris, having been relocated from Metz during the political conflicts of 1870, Chaumont took her under his wing, and she embraced the programme of formation that he had drawn up from the writings of de Sales. Then, with a small nucleus of similarly devout

military wives, Madame Carré launched an informal association, the Daughters of Francis de Sales, whose members

> ... aspire to evangelical holiness in a spirit of Christian
> simplicity. To do so, they must never forget that the begin-
> ning, way and end of the Christian life is absolute union
> with Our Lord Jesus Christ. They strive to overcome even
> the smallest faults and willing imperfections, ... they will
> be renewed by the awareness of their own humility, and
> love and practice, as they are able, the three evangelical
> virtues of religious life [faith, hope, and charity].[48]

With Chaumont, this wife and mother from Metz organised
a system of formation which involved 'probations,' courses of
reading and spiritual practice centred upon the virtues practised in the Salesian mode, especially humility, patience,
fidelity, prudence, modesty and responsiveness to the Holy
Spirit.[49]

Like Chaumont and Ségur, who deemed himself the 'grand-
father' of the Daughters, Caroline Carré was filled with the
desire to spread the Salesian vision of a world of hearts. She
expended her effort, not only in service of the Daughters, but
attempted to found a society of priests steeped in Salesian
spirituality for the express purpose of providing direction for
the laywomen's group. And as Chaumont envisioned other
associations for the promotion of Christian values in the home,
so she envisioned an association for the moral education of
members of the servant classes. Not all of these ambitious
plans for the establishment of a world of divine and human
hearts were realised or lasted long. Nonetheless, the Daughters of St Francis de Sales flourished, their ranks swelled in
the 1880s with devout religious expelled from their convents
by government decree who wished to continue their lives of
evangelical perfection without formal vows or a recognisable
religious habit.

From its origins in the Salesian Pentecost, the Daughters of
Francis de Sales has become a worldwide organisation. In
the twenty-first century it remains a lay organisation, now

canonically established, that operates under the title The Association of St Francis de Sales. It promotes the same goals of sanctification in the Salesian spirit and employs essentially the same, though updated, practices of spiritual formation as it did at its foundation. A late twentieth-century brochure articulates the particular spiritual emphasis of this branch of the Salesian tradition.

> St Francis de Sales accepted as basic the universal call to holiness taught by Christ and suggested the means by which we might attain it. It was from his spirit that our founder, Canon Chaumont, drew inspiration when composing a rule of life ... the rule, adapted to today's lifestyle, without diverging from the original intention of the foundation, proposes to Christians: to live according to the Spirit of Jesus, to live the Gospel in the Church and in the world, to live the Gospel as disciples of St Francis de Sales, to live the Gospel with Mary, the Mother of the Church and our Mother ...
>
> Francis de Sales leads us to the perfection of love through: confidence in the goodness of God; humility and gentleness of heart, source of our courage, sincerity and spiritual 'listening'; obedience which is freely consented to through love and which gives its character to duty of state; chastity practiced according to each one's state in life, which is the element of purification and the factor of good balance; poverty which makes one free and available.[50]

When in July of 1881 Gaspard Mermillod preached the sermon at Ségur's funeral at the church of Notre Dame in Paris, there was not a dry eye in the overflowing congregation. Comparing the ever-inventive Ségur to Francis de Sales, the Cardinal's words were perhaps somewhat flowery, but they expressed the sentiments of those present: that day they marked the passing of one of the great servants of their generation whose unceasing and generous apostolic activity left an indelible mark on individual hearts and on the heart of the Catholic community at large.[51]

THE *SPIRITUAL DIRECTORY*:
OBLATES AND OBLATE SISTERS

> What is your mission? It is that of religious: to save souls, to give them a strong foundation in an authentic and solid Christian life. The holier you become, the more influence you will have on souls who will come to you. The best means, however, for acquiring this holiness is to unite yourself to God by a faithful practice of the Directory of St Francis de Sales.[52]
>
> Fr Louis Brisson

The revolutions – both political and industrial – of the modern world left their mark on the fabric of nineteenth-century society. In some regions after the Restoration, Catholic observance was fervent and widespread. In other regions, knowledge and practice of the faith was waning.[53] In all regions, the movement of populations from the countryside to the town and the swift transition from an agricultural to an industrial economy created social havoc. The shape of the resurgent Catholic community was contoured by these social realities. In the diocese of Troyes in northeastern France that resurgence was marked in its Salesian character. The practice of the Catholic faith for many in Troyes was lax and tepid, yet it was there that several of the brightest fires of the Salesian Pentecost burst forth. At the heart of this kindling of hearts were three figures: Marie de Sales Chappuis (1793–1875), Superior of the Troyes Visitation, Fr Louis Brisson (1817–1908) who, with Mother Chappuis, founded the Oblates of St Francis de Sales, and Léonie Aviat (1844–1914), who with Father Brisson was co-founder of the Oblate Sisters of St Francis de Sales.

The 'Good Mother'

The network of devout Catholics who saw in Francis de Sales the perfect model and patron of re-evangelisation was widespread. Monseigneur de Ségur in Paris, Bishop Mermillod in

Savoy and Don Bosco in the Piedmont were aware of each other's apostolic efforts as they were aware of the works under the Salesian aegis that were developing in Troyes. And as many of these founders had suffered from the suppression of religion, so too the remarkable woman who was the spark that ignited the spiritual fires in Troyes was, as a child, formed by the dark spectre of religious repression.[54] Marie-Thérèse Chappuis was born at Soyhières, a mountain village in the Swiss Jura, which during the Revolution had been annexed to France. An early memory recalled by her biographers is of her discovery at the age of four of the clandestine midnight Masses celebrated in the family homes by her uncle, the former curé of Soyhières who was forced to remain in hiding during the day for fear of discovery. Her parents were from an ancient Catholic family of the region and raised their eleven children (of whom Marie-Thérèse was number seven) in an intensely devotional atmosphere: of the eleven children, six later become priests or religious. Early on, young Marie was introduced to the Salesian spirit at the Visitation school in Fribourg, Switzerland, where she boarded for several years. She even entered that monastic community as a postulant in 1811 but, because of homesickness, stayed only a few months. Three years later she entered again and remained. Thus began the remarkable career of the woman who would come to see herself as an Apostle of the Salesian spirit through whom the world would be reformed. This high calling was in fact defined by the kenotic (self-emptying) pattern of the Christ life that the Visitation founders had promoted. In a mystical reverie during her novitiate that recalls both Jane de Chantal and Margaret Mary Alacoque, Marie-Thérèse, now Marie de Sales, experienced a radical transformation of heart.

> My heart has been opened wide. There has been placed in it an inspiration which shows one clearly the wishes of the Lord, that he wants to direct my whole being ... My whole being will be destroyed in every way. God ought to be known – his will is that his life in me serve that

purpose. Here is how I shall be. After he sends a bright and powerful fire which must change the human creature, everything in my life will be for that purpose.[55]

Indeed, Francis had preached to his Visitandine spiritual daughters of their apostolic calling, words that they faithfully recorded in the *Conferences*.

Oh what grace does God bestow upon you! He makes you apostles not in dignity but in office and merit. You will not preach, it is true, for your sex does not permit it, although indeed St Magdalene and her sister Martha did so, but you will not cease to exercise the apostolic office by communicating your way of life.[56]

For Marie Chappuis, Visitation life would in fact follow the pattern that was shown to her at the very onset of her religious commitment. Due to her deep grasp of Salesian principles and her uncommon leadership ability, within a year she was sent to Metz to re-establish the Visitation convent there, then made novice mistress at Fribourg, and from there sent to restore the Salesian spirit to the monastery at Troyes, which had been disbanded in 1789 and reorganised in 1807. By the time Marie de Sales Chappuis arrived, the convent was definitely in need of a visionary leader. For several decades previously the community had been under ecclesiastical interdict on account of Jansenist tendencies, and the flavour of these persisted. In addition, community life of the Visitation model was in disarray. The young superior, in typically Salesian fashion, was able to win the hearts of all and transform the Troyes community into the sort of place where a union of hearts could reign. For most of her long years, with the exception of an interval when she provided leadership for the Paris Visitation, Marie de Sales served the Troyes monastery. She came to be known as the 'Good Mother' both by her sisters in religion as well as by others outside who were affected by her many works.

The Good Mother was steeped in Salesian wisdom: indeed, she was commonly believed to be the authentic interpreter of

Salesian teaching in her day.[57] But, as with any rich and complex spiritual tradition, each interpreter internalises the teachings in a unique way and emphasises certain aspects. Marie de Sales Chappuis was thus the source of several distinctive sayings and practices that grew out of her profound reverence for the *Spiritual Directory* of Francis de Sales, adherence to which, in her mind, was the surest way to embody the Salesian Spirit, which is simply to 'Live Jesus'.

The *Spiritual Directory*

In the course of establishing guidelines for the new community he was founding with Jane de Chantal, Francis de Sales had written a variety of directories to govern everyday life. There were directories for the novice mistress, directories for the performance of the Little Office of Our Lady and other cere- monies, directories for the various officers of the monastery and what was known as the *Spiritual Directory for Daily Actions*. The latter contained numerous practices to be per- formed throughout the day. These exercises especially emphasised the intention with which a sister should approach such common activities as rising, hearing Mass, practising an examination of conscience, eating in the refectory, keeping silence and going to bed. These were formative practices designed to habituate each community member to infusing each moment with a sense of divine presence and purpose. Not all individual Visitandines or monasteries have given such emphasis to the *Spiritual Directory* as did Marie de Sales Chappuis. For her, faithful practice of the *Directory* was the key to the spiritual life. In this, she was not unique among her contemporaries. Others in the nineteenth century engaged in refounding religion after the Revolution emphasised the sanctifying power of the Rule for religious life. The Good Mother treated the *Directory* as others did the Rule.

I repeat, that without the spirit of the *Directory*, one can never be enlightened so as to fully comprehend it, but

with that spirit, the good God will give us light moment
by moment . . . At the hour of death, God will only demand
of us our fidelity to what is contained in this little book.
The *Directory* gives the manner of doing everything. It is
by observing the letter that we acquire the spirit, and it
is by this spirit of the *Directory* that each one will cover
herself as with a mantle, taking another spirit than her
own. If each one has the same spirit, she has also the
same inclinations, and that is called living in union. To be
a religious in heart, we must do what the *Directory*
teaches. It came from the Heart of God; it has been sanctified by thousands, and thousands have been sanctified by
it. It can never grow old.[58]

It was especially the direction of intention – the practice at
the onset of every action, both inner and outer, of asking for
God's grace and offering to God all the good that might come
from the action – that expressed the purpose of the *Directory*.
That purpose was the union of God's heart with the human
heart. When the Good Mother spoke of 'The Way' she was
referring to this deep union, especially as it was experienced
as trust in and dependence upon the will of God's good pleasure
known in the present moment. And when Marie de Sales
admonished her spiritual charges to *couper court* ('cut it
short'), she was advising that they might be freed from self-
indulgence, self-pity, or self-absorption by turning their minds
and hearts back to God in the present moment.

The generous liberty of spirit so central to Salesian spirituality – the ability to live gracefully between what Francis
termed the 'two wills of God' – is grounded in a profound sense
of trust. The Good Mother, like the founders she emulated,
rested on the breast of Jesus with a childlike confidence. Her
Pensées record her particular expression of this truth.

Let us leave ourselves absolutely in God's hands. Let us
say with all our heart: 'I am sure of God.'

As regards myself, I am indeed sure of him. This I can
truly declare. I desire that this assurance should reach

His Sacred Heart and say plainly and simply; 'I rely on you, without knowing how, only I know that I rely on you.'[59]

The trust she felt was closely linked with an embrace of the will of God's good pleasure, a spiritual posture that Jane de Chantal herself had cultivated.

> I don't want to lose any opportunity to ask God to manifest His goodness, for that would be depriving Him of what He loves best. Being what He is, God can do nothing but what is good; it is God's nature to do good. He wishes to do us good for His own sake. The good He wishes to do us in Himself shows His infinite mercy.
>
> We can never comprehend what the goodness of God really is, His attributes are beyond our understanding and we make great mistakes about them; therefore we must simply say 'yes' to all He asks of us and leave His unsearchable goodness to act as it will.[60]
>
> I am content, O Lord, to wait, my happiness is to submit to your good pleasure. I am just as pleased to be deprived of what I want as to have it; all I desire is to wait for your good pleasure. Possessing what I want ceases to please me if it is not ordained by Your Will.[61]

The inner serenity expressed in Marie's personal *pensées* was the fertile ground out of which her flourishing apostolic works grew.[62]

Marie de Sales saw her role as a transformer of hearts not only in her community, but also in the world about her, and the means by which she accomplished this were astonishingly creative and varied. With the *Directory* as her guide, she provided venerable leadership for the monastery. She was also instrumental in reforming the boarding school that the community operated for the education of young women; the convent-like atmosphere upon which she insisted nurtured in the boarders the solid little virtues necessary for Christian women to live faithfully in the world. Under her leadership, the vision of Francis' *Introduction to the Devout Life* permeated the school instruction.

The Association of Francis de Sales, promoted so vigorously by Monseigneur de Ségur, soon engaged the Good Mother. With the aid of the boarding school students, she supported the spread of the lay movement. Through her efforts, by 1860 there were 6,000 associates in 35 parishes in the Troyes region engaged in the study of the writings of Francis de Sales. In addition, the plight of the poor did not escape her notice: young girls newly arriving in the city to seek work in the factories were often in desperate need. Under Mother Chappuis' sponsorship, five houses that met these needs were founded, staffed first by volunteers, then by a religious community of women, the Oblate Sisters of St Francis de Sales, with roots in the Visitation school. Nor were priests and prelates ignored. Father de Malet, to whom the Good Mother gave spiritual direction, became the confessor and guide to several bishops and a host of priests whom he in turn formed in the Salesian spirit. And, through her influence, the moral theology of the recently canonised St Alphonsus Liguori was introduced in the Troyes seminary. Most memorably, Mother de Sales Chappuis was responsible for the creation of a men's congregation, the Oblates of St Francis de Sales. It was this task – to which for decades she urged the monastery's chaplain and confessor Louis Brisson – that she believed was her life's work.

Louis Brisson[63]

Brisson was raised in a devout family in the village of Plancy, and as an adolescent had been exposed at close hand to the anti-clericalism that raged during the 1830 uprisings. His entry into the seminary was thus a natural one for the serious student who excelled in literature and the sciences. Indeed, Louis' fascination with scientific invention never left him. He would continue to experiment and explore throughout his life; the development of an astronomical clock occupied him for decades. In 1840, after a time as professor of science at the seminary, the young priest served as catechist, confessor, and teacher of science, religion and literature at the Troyes Visitation boarding school. There he was deeply influenced by Marie de Sales Chappuis, and their partnership would eventually bear fruit in a number of apostolic works. In 1843 he became chaplain to the monastery community itself and took lodgings next to the convent where he brought his ageing parents to live. In both positions, at the school and at the convent itself, Brisson was immersed in the Salesian spirit, a spirit that Mother Marie de Sales had so carefully instilled. His Visitation experience increased the love for the Savoyard saint that Louis had first acquired in seminary.

Brisson saw himself, as did many Catholics emerging from contemporary political and religious turmoil, as championing the true faith over and against both the rigid religious Jansenism and the irreligious secularism of the day. To counter this, the faith he taught was Francis de Sales' devout humanism with its generous vision of a world of divine and human hearts. At its core, Salesian spirituality is about living Jesus, about a transformation of heart occurring in the intimacy of heart to heart prayer that, in its turn, transforms the hearts of others. Louis Brisson, with Marie de Sales, often referred to this process as 'Reprinting the Gospel'. They taught that one must 'Live Jesus' or 'Reprint the Gospel' in all aspects of life. It was especially through prayer, work, evangelisation, and sacrifice that the transformation was effected.

> It is not enough to read the Gospel in order to understand it. We must live it. The Gospel is the true story of the Word of God living on earth among men. We must produce a New Edition of this Gospel among men by prayer, work, preaching and sacrifice, four points in all.
>
> We reprint the Gospel, first of all, by prayer . . . [by] prayer, man gives himself to God in every way without reserve . . .
>
> May all that is in us and of us find its way into our prayer, unite itself to God and abandon itself to His love![64]

We reprint the Gospel, secondly, by means of work. We must reprint the Gospel and reprint it page by page without omitting anything. Now Our Lord came upon earth and passed thirty years in manual labor . . . It is precisely because He was a workingman, because He worked with His hands, that He knew this language of divine science so much elevated above human thought, the language of union with the will of God. He began by doing manual labor. Without doubt, all of us cannot work with our hands, but in our life there is always a little manual labor. There is a library to keep in order, a helping hand to be given, a little gardening to be done, a little tidying up or arranging to be done. You are in charge of a class: this often requires some material care. I very strongly recommend devotion to manual labor. God has attached great graces to manual labor.[65]

The third evangelical task . . . is the evangelization of the nations, the preaching of our Lord . . . The preaching of the Gospel was one of the principal reasons for His coming. We, therefore, should reprint the Gospel also by our preaching. All of us should preach. Those who work with their hands as well as those who are occupied with our exterior works, those who conduct classes as well as those who teach by example, those who direct souls as well as those who are assigned to the ministry of the pulpit, all of us should preach. We should preach in a practical way. We should teach our neighbor, if not by our words, at least by our actions.[66]

The fourth thing in the Gospel is sacrifice. The Word made flesh prayed in order to teach us how to pray. He worked. He preached. Finally, He suffered. These are the four conditions necessary to reprint the Gospel. The fourth and last page is the Passion of Our Lord . . .

The Good Mother points out as an habitual sacrifice the *couper court*. When we suffer pain, we must cut short all reflections, all murmurings and say, 'I accept it.' When we are tempted to pride or sensuality, we must cut short again. Someone causes you pain or expresses disdain for you. Why do you stop there? 'Why do you listen to your own thoughts?' says St Francis de Sales. *Couper court!*

Sacrifice, thus understood and practised, is extremely pleasing to God. Cut short whatever binds you to your own will, whatever makes you look back, whatever enchains you and holds you captive.

By practicing the *couper court*, you acquire a considerable amount of strength and energy . . . Day by day, hour by hour, you will develop the habit of sacrifice. And when a formal order of God will ask of you something difficult, something which will seem impossible to nature, you will accept it completely and courageously.[67]

This distinctive, yet utterly Salesian, vision of living Jesus Fr Brisson taught to all those with whom he came into contact. Particularly striking is the emphasis on manual work and the dignity of the labourer. In this sensibility the Troyes Salesians reflect Catholic thought of the era, which would be officially promulgated at the end of the nineteenth century by Pope Leo XIII. Leo's *Rerum Novarum* (On the Condition of Labour) is the first of the great encyclicals of modern Catholic social teaching that proclaim the dignity of each person which, in turn, necessitates humane working conditions and a just wage. Fr Brisson and Marie de Sales Chappuis' vision of a world of hearts included the hearts of the working class.

From the beginning of their association, the Good Mother felt that Louis Brisson was called by God to give himself to the encouragement of the reign of hearts on earth. In fact, she had a very specific vision of what she believed he was called to do: establish the community of men that Francis himself had not lived long enough to found. Her assurance, founded on her own intimate communications with Jesus, and her constant urgings in that direction, frankly unnerved the young chaplain. For thirty years he listened wearily to her prophetic entreaties, but always assured her that he had neither the ability nor the inclination for such a momentous undertaking. In part, he felt a contemplative call and tested that call for a time in a Carthusian monastery, a hermit community where silence was broken only by the strains of sung liturgical prayer. Eventually, the Good Mother's prophecies, or her persistence, would win the day.[68]

Meanwhile, Fr Brisson's days were full enough with his duties at the Visitation. In addition, he had been drawn into the momentum of the plans emanating from Paris for the establishment of the Association of St Francis de Sales. With Marie de Sales' encouragement, he spearheaded the efforts in the Troyes diocese. In its first year alone the Association enlisted 3,000 members. The work of the Association was multifold. It sponsored among its projects a study club for soldiers, a mission club, a Catholic Action club dedicated to bringing people back or newly to the sacraments, and a neighbourhood club for factory girls. The latter apostolate was eventually to give birth to an entirely new religious community, the Oblate Sisters of St Francis de Sales.

Léonie Aviat[69]

Among the graduates of the Visitation school was one young woman from Troyes, Léonie Aviat, whose life would intertwine intimately with those of Louis Brisson and the Good Mother. Léonie, the second daughter of a well-regarded merchant couple in Sézanne, first met Brisson when he, as chaplain at the school where her sister was a boarder, made a visit to her family. At the age of eleven she entered the school herself and stayed until she was sixteen. These were profoundly formative years. She loved the school, the chaplain, and the Good Mother; under their tutelage she was instructed in Salesian principles. She so loved her Visitation experience that twice, after returning home, she broached the idea of becoming a nun. Her not overly observant parents' plan for her was marriage. However, Léonie kept in contact with the school and Fr Brisson and continued to make yearly retreats at the monastery, nurturing the hope that some day she could respond to the call she felt to give herself to God.

When she turned twenty-one and was legally free to make her own decisions, Léonie did reject her parents' dream. But her future turned out differently from her imaginings. Brisson and the Good Mother held in common a deep concern for the young women who flooded into the city looking for work in an increasingly industrialised society. Few ministries were operated with them in mind; clubs and programmes were available for working-class boys but not for their sisters. The Visitation chaplain and superior therefore purchased a house on the rue de Terrasse that housed fifty girls and sponsored Sunday spiritual conferences that drew many others. Volunteer administrators were recruited for the programme. Soon it was clear that a more permanent leadership was necessary. In 1866, with former schoolmate Lucie Canuet, Léonie went on an eight-day retreat with the Good Mother to discern her future, aided in prayer by Fr Brisson. At the end of the retreat, she immediately embarked on the road that would lead to a 'religious institute whose members, drawing inspirations from the holy apostle of the Chablais, would fill the role of mother and teacher for these working girls'.[70] Léonie and Lucie moved into a dwelling fittingly called 'the little Gallery House' in memory of the donated building that in 1610 had housed the first Visitation community.

The new community, which became known as the Oblate Sisters of St Francis de Sales, was nurtured by the Good Mother. They were welcomed into the monastery parlour for advice, and the assistant in the novitiate was assigned the task of guiding them in the practical application of the Visitation Rule that had been adapted for an active ministry. At the centre of the spiritual life of the Oblate Sisters was the practice of the *Spiritual Directory*, which was to provide the template for their own way of 'Reprinting the Gospel'. The practice of being open to the grace present in every moment, of offering in advance every good thing to the good God, and of peacefully accepting in advance all difficulty as coming from

that same good God – the direction of intention – sustained
Léonie in her often arduous calling. Years later she would say,

> I still remember the words the Good Mother said to us
> one day on this subject: 'The faithful practice of the Direc-
> tion of Intention is the first rung on the ladder that will
> make us attain sanctity.' She had been so faithful to this
> article that she knew its reward.[71]

In Salesian fashion, this same interior practice undergirded
both the life of the cloistered Visitandine and the very engaged
life of service led by an Oblate Sister.

> My children, [wrote the Good Mother] you are not called
> to say the office for the moment. Your principal occupation
> is work. Give yourself to it as graciously as possible. Go
> to your work when the clock chimes: Set out joyfully
> according to our Rule, as if you were going to say the office
> and make meditation, because for you, work is a continual
> meditation.[72]

Léonie was given the name Frances de Sales Aviat in a
ceremony of consecration performed by Gaspard Mermillod, at
that time auxiliary Bishop of Lausanne, Fribourg, and Geneva.
From then until her death forty-six years later, Sister, then
Mother, Frances de Sales would labour at the helm of her
rapidly expanding order. The community responded to the
needs of the people and engaged in a variety of works including
the various works of the Oblate men's community that Fr
Brisson would found. The course of these ministries was often
thwarted by war, shifts in politics and government policies,
and continued religious persecution. Throughout it all, Léonie
looked to her patrons for aid. Frightened and exhausted during
the terrors of the Franco-Prussian war, she prayed,

> St Francis de Sales, you have chosen me to be at the head
> of this little troop; give me your spirit and heart. Ask Jane
> de Chantal to give me all her firmness and, at the same
> time, her compassion and heart for my neighbor,

forgetfulness of self, and a great simplicity with our good Father. Give me your union with God that knows how to do everything with God and nothing without Him.[73]

The saintly founders must have smiled upon her request, as Leonie's internalisation of the Salesian spirit was in fact profound. Her sense of the graciousness of God and God's providential care never wavered, even in the face of great challenges, and she continued to guide her community with the distinctive Salesian combination of gentleness and zeal that wins hearts. 'Confidence attracts confidence but it does not command. . . . One must have great prudence, charity and discretion. Young people must feel that you respect their little secrets', she would write.[74]

In the same manner, her inner life was shaped by the unceasing desire for heart to heart intimacy with God. In her retreat journals she recorded this characteristic prayer:

> My God . . . may I have no other desire now but to apply myself to the practice of the *Directory* and a complete union with Our Lord. May my obedience have no limits! May my devotedness to souls know no bounds! . . . O Mary, may I go, delivered from all my fears, to you and to Jesus with the heart of a child, the heart of an Oblate Sister of St Francis de Sales.[75]

And like her spiritual mentor, Léonie experienced an intimacy that was characterised by trust and surrender. The summit of the spiritual life was ' . . . to place oneself in the hands of God and our good father, like a little child who doesn't know any-thing, but who tries confidently to do all she is told'.[76]

The Oblates of St Francis de Sales[77]

The Oblate Sisters would not be the only religious community that Louis Brisson would help found. The Good Mother never allowed him to forget her vision that placed him at the head of a men's congregation dedicated to the dissemination of the

spirit of St Francis de Sales. Encouraged by others, especially
Bishop Mermillod, by his own love of Salesian spirituality and
by his growing conviction that Marie de Sales indeed had
prophetic vision, the reality of a community of men – the
Oblates of St Francis de Sales – came to Brisson's full focused
attention.[78] The immediate need that finally prompted the
creation of the community was the education of young men. A
school, which became known as St Bernard's College, was the
first apostolate Brisson and his early recruits undertook. Given
the social conditions, it was not easy work for, on the same
day that the foundation of a projected new school building was
dug, the Franco-German War was declared. There was intense
opposition to the undertaking, yet Brisson persisted and
gradually the vision the Good Mother had announced some
thirty years earlier emerged. Eventually, funding was pro-
cured, more vocations for the congregation presented
themselves, students came, and requests from nearby dioceses
for schools and priests to staff them flooded in. As the congregation grew, so did its ministries; beyond the schools the
Oblates extended their care to working-class children and to
the work of preaching. Throughout it all, the spiritual vision
of a world of divine–human hearts sustained the new congregation. The 'Way' about which the Good Mother and Louis
Brisson spoke was the way of Christ followed in the spirit of
Francis de Sales and realised through faithful adherence to
the practices of the *Spiritual Directory*.[79]

> All religious orders have their own spirit and particular
> qualities drawn from special practices designed to achieve
> them. The Carthusians are men of silence and solitude,
> the Trappists men of manual work and mortification.
>   What must our spirit be? Our methods are not those of
> the penitential orders. Our founder has laid out a sure
> and direct path for us – the *Directory*. It is the *Directory*
> that is our method, our reason for being, and which pro-
> vides us our particular quality.
>   The *Directory* is self-renunciation in each action and

moment of the day, it is union with the Savior, it is the Savior's hand which directs each of us on the path. By practicing the *Directory* one not only becomes formed into a true religious but from faithful observance will receive illumination to clarify the intellect and gain a sure knowledge and grasp of the highest dogmatic and moral truths.

With the practice of the *Directory* we will become more complete than if we followed another method, no matter how trustworthy, pious or excellent it might be. Other approaches emphasise the regulation of external actions. Our approach reaches into the depth of our being and captures our heart and soul and trains our aspirations to unite them to God.

The *Directory* created St Francis de Sales. Our holy patron began to practise it in his youth before giving it to the Visitandines and it was the *Directory* which made the Saint into the true image of the Saviour here on earth.

The fruits of the *Directory* are peace of soul, the repose of the Spirit in God without disquiet, or restlessness . . . the *Directory* is a pure and easy route that provides peace of soul and union with God.[80]

It was Brisson's belief that the practice of the direction of intention, so central to the *Directory*, was the means through which a habitual sense of the presence of God was acquired. This sense was not merely psychological but spiritual, and effected an actual indwelling of the divine presence. Quite commonplace on its surface, this teaching pointed to a mystical union with the divine.

This doctrine [the direction of intention] made a deep impression on me, even in my first years of theology. One of my professors brought it to my attention. 'Notice,' he said, 'how the teaching of St Francis de Sales is conformed to loftiest theology.' The Incarnation is God-made-man, but it is not only the God-man Who was destined to be united to the Divinity. In the divine plan, not only is the Divinity united to one man in order to form the God-man, but Divinity also wishes the Incarnation to apply to all. It wishes to communicate with the whole human race. It wishes to become incarnate in all, not hypostatically, of course, but in no less efficacious manner in all who are willing and prepared. Our Lord is God and He acts and works in us.

While the Incarnation was applied to one human nature only, it has in reality spread to all the members of the Mystical Body of Our Lord [the Church]. The blood that flows through the Sacred Heart of Jesus passes through every part of the Mystical Body.[81]

This habitual sense of living Jesus remains a linchpin of spiritual formation of the Oblate congregation which in the twenty-first century ministers in varied apostolates around the world, including education, missions, and pastoral ministry in parishes, hospitals and the military.

ENGLISH ADMIRERS AND PIOUS LADIES

She was nobly loyal – loyal to her community and its precious traditions, loyal to every one of her sisters, loyal to the Order, to its Holy Founders, to its Rules and Customs. 'God has placed in the hands of our fidelity the preservation of the Institute' was a favorite maxim of hers, frequently on her lips, and always clearly expressed in the whole conduct of her religious life ... Sister Evangelista's influence was not obtrusive – it worked silently, yet surely, through what she was, through her beautiful deeply spiritual character – simple, sincere, frank, guileless as a child.[82]

1922 death letter of Sr Evangelista Prince,
St Louis Visitation

The dynamic vision of a world of hearts first articulated at the dawn of the seventeenth century by a French-speaking Savoyard and a Frenchwoman from Burgundy would not long be confined to populations speaking the Romance languages.

The English-speaking world would also have its Salesian followers.[83] Even during his own lifetime, Francis' writings became known across the English channel. King James I of England himself expressed a desire to meet the author of the admirable *Introduction to the Devout Life*. Learning of this Francis, ever the missionary, replied that he would give his life a thousand times over to bring England back to the Roman church but if he were to do that the Pope would need to send him.

The Savoyard bishop's desire for the island's conversion was shared by others, especially the English who remained loyal to the Catholic faith and who, beginning with the reign of Henry VIII, were socially marginalised, legally discriminated against and even vigorously persecuted. The English recusant Church maintained its vitality underground and was nurtured by educational institutions abroad; the Jesuits established a seminary at Douai, French Flanders (later transferred to Rheims), and a college in Rome for the training of English Catholics. The Salesian legacy was transmitted there. Throughout the seventeenth and eighteenth centuries contact between the persecuted English Church and Catholics on the continent was constant.

English Franciscan and Benedictine monasteries that had been suppressed were able to establish foundations in the Low Countries and France. As a result, the first English translation of de Sales' *Conferences* was made by an English Benedictine nun in an exiled community abroad. Numerous direct English translations of the *Introduction*, printed in Antwerp, Louvain, Rouen, Paris, Douai and Rheims appeared. The extent to which English spiritual consciousness was steeped in Salesian thought is suggested by the way in which the late seventeenth-century 'poetry of meditation' or 'metaphysical poetry', with which the names Herbert, Crawshaw, Vaughn and Donne are linked, is dependent on his writing. Francis' methods of meditation outlined in the *Introduction* brought together the senses, emotions, imagination and intellectual faculties to create spiritual insight. It was this method, along with methods promoted by other early modern Catholic devotional writers, that shaped both English religious and literary sensibilities.[84]

Further English–continental connections were often strengthened by the marriage practices of the royal families of Europe whose conjugal unions were forged with a view to political advantage rather than religious compatibility. It was Jesuit Claude la Colombière, Margaret Mary Alacoque's confessor and soul friend, who in 1675 was appointed as court preacher to Catholic Mary of Modena (Marie-Beatrix d'Este), and who first offered a Mass in honour of the Sacred Heart on English soil. Three years later, as anti-Catholic sentiment resurfaced, Claude was imprisoned and his health fatally compromised. Mary of Modena, wife of the Duke of York (later James II) was not only Catholic but an admirer of the Visitation Order. It appears as though she had plans that never materialised to found an English Visitation. Queen Mary had close ties with the Visitation monastery at Chaillot near Paris, a convent founded previously by another exiled English Catholic queen, her mother-in-law, Henrietta Marie, widow of Charles I. In fact, the hearts of these two queens as well as the hearts of James II and his daughter by Mary of Modena, Marie-Louise, were all preserved and venerated at the Chaillot community.[85]

The Visitation was finally established on English soil at the beginning of the nineteenth century due to the efforts of a Mrs Turnstall of Lancashire whose recusant ancestors counted among them a martyr. Three Visitation sisters from the monastery of Rouen set up a foundation in Acton, near London in 1804. English Catholic applicants were waiting in the wings, nurtured in their faith by the indefatigable Jesuits. Characteristic is the story of Mary Weld whose family chaplain was Jesuit Father Nicolas Grou, one of the outstanding spiritual guides of the time. Mary, who became Sister Mary de Sales, served as the first English Superior of the community. In their turn, her younger sister Clare and her niece Fanny Vaughan also became distinguished superiors of the Order. The Acton community moved to Somerset and in 1816 founded a confraternity of the Sacred Heart, relocated in 1896 to Westbury-on-Trim, then moved to Harrow-on-the-Hill in London, and finally after World War II, relocated to Waldron in Sussex. The English connection was a fruitful one for the spread of the Salesian vision. The sisters of Harrow-on-the-Hill produced a number of English language publications including Jane de Chantal's selected letters, Francis' letters, a translation of the *Treatise*, and original studies of Visitandine notables.[86]

Dom Mackey and the Library of St Francis de Sales

Resurgent nineteenth century English Catholicism consisted of a small, tight-knit group with the Visitation and the Salesian vision very much at its core. Well-known recusant family names dominate the registry of the confraternity of the Sacred Heart, and the Visitation archives. One of the members at Harrow-on-the-Hill, who received the name Frances Margaret when she entered the community in 1866, was the younger sister of Henry Benedict Mackey (1846–1906), a Benedictine priest whose influence in the dissemination of the Salesian spirituality in the English-speaking world cannot be underestimated.[87] Henry and his five siblings were born to a cultured English Catholic family of Erdington. Trained in France at St Edmund's College in Douai, an institution founded to serve beleaguered English Catholics, Henry entered the Benedictine novitiate at St Michael's in Hereford. There he met John Cuthbert Hedley, OSB, later Bishop of Newport, who suggested to the young monk what would become his life's work – the life and works of St Francis de Sales. Indeed, Henry and St Francis were to be intimates for the remainder of the former's life and he would be an outstanding example of the admiration with which some British Benedictines regarded de Sales.[88] He began by reading the *Conferences*, then moved to translating and preparing articles and pamphlets about Francis. The first article to appear in print was occasioned by the 1877 Bull of Pius IX that conferred the title Doctor of the Church on the much-revered saint. Several articles followed, all in the *Dublin Review*, which reveal the depth of Mackey's familiarity with the Salesian founder's life and thought. Indeed, he entered into a lively and sometimes critical conversation with other English-speaking authors who had already written about or translated the words of the Savoyard.

In 1882 Mackey began a correspondence with the Visitation in Annecy where a team of sisters were preparing a new (and what remains the critical) edition of Francis' writings. Eventually the Benedictine was relieved of his parochial assignments and spent twelve years shuttling between Annecy and Rome (where he frequently represented the Benedictine Order), involved in all aspects of the preparation and publication of this multi-volumed edition. To this task he brought his erudition and sound scholarly methods; later commentators have acknowledged his contribution to the edition's critical character. For Mackey the enterprise was more than a scholarly one, and his aim in the collaboration was

> . . . to publish all the writings of the Holy doctor, to reproduce them in the integrity of the original texts with all the care and typographical perfection merited by a teaching of so elevated an order, in a word, to make Francis de Sales known such as he depicted himself in his works and such as he is offered to the admiration of the Church of God.[89]

The Church of God in England was not, in Dom Mackey's mind, to be cut off from the admirable Salesian vision for want of fluency in the French language. Perhaps the Benedictine's greatest achievement is the work he did in the preparation of the English language *Library of St Francis de Sales*.[90] Mackey himself prepared most of the translations and wrote introductions or prefaces to the majority of the volumes, even the several that were published posthumously. Interestingly, the English *Library* does not contain a translation of the ever-popular *Introduction to the Devout Life*: perhaps Mackey felt there were already so many apt English translations available (he did recommend one by a Father Richard). The Benedictine admirer of the Salesian vision has been criticised by later translators, especially by those who have tackled the *Treatise on the Love of God*, for his rather stiff and literal rendering of the original French.[91] Indeed, he and the Annecy Visitandines had their genteel disagreements when he added his labours to theirs in the preparation of the Annecy edition (his *mentalité* was too English and not French enough for the sisters). His gifts as a translator aside, Mackey's contribution to the spread of Salesian spirituality in the English-speaking world should not be underestimated. Moreover, the analysis and interpretation that he offered in his prefaces are accurate and still helpful.[92] His treatment of the *Treatise*, a dense and often daunting work, is sympathetic, penetrating and rooted in Francis' own spirit. For Mackey understood this masterwork not only as a work of theory, but as a book to be meditated upon and prayed with, a book that can open the heart of the reader to the unfathomable love poured out from the heart of God.

In his articles Dom Mackey affirmed that St Francis' sweet and appealing 'art of devotion' was a sure path for those living in the world. The practice of the little virtues he saw as culminating in the 'virtue of virtues' – doing the will of God. The special character of Mackey summed up the special character of Salesian virtue in a remark about mortification which, 'like every other virtue, resides in the heart and will and must go from within outwards'.[93] For the Benedictine admirer, the life of devotion outlined in the *Introduction* could not be separated from 'the profoundist science of the spiritual life' discovered in the *Treatise*. His commentary on that text focused on the will of God's good pleasure as 'a disposition, a general sense of waiting'. It also emphasised Francis' deep assimilation of both the theory and practice of the contemplative tradition which Francis knew 'in his own blessed soul, and in hers [Jane de Chantal] who was, as he says, "one soul with him".' The cultivation of this open-hearted disposition takes place by the simple entrustment (*simple rémise*) of oneself into the arms of God.

Against commentators (primarily Protestant), who felt that Francis' appealing spirituality could easily be detached from his Catholic theology, Mackey was firm. From the vantage point of one whose faith community had overcome fearsome odds to remain loyal to Rome, the Benedictine underscored the Savoyard's Catholicity: 'He who preaches with love preaches sufficiently against heresy.'[94]

The Salesian Spirit in America

The Catholic population in the English colonies of the New World and the American new Republic was not large. But the Salesian legacy was nevertheless strikingly evident there. A case in point might be the experience of Elizabeth Ann Seton, foundress of the American Sisters of Charity. As a young Episcopalian widow, struggling with her grief, Elizabeth had been given a copy of the *Introduction to the Devout Life* by her late husband's Italian Catholic business partners. The inviting Salesian world of hearts joined to the warmth of Italian Catholicism won the American widow's heart and was crucial in her conversion. Struggling to come to grips with the cost of such a conversion, Elizabeth wrote to her Italian friends:

> I read the promises given to St Peter and the 6th chapter of John everyday and then ask God if I can offend him by believing those express words. I read my dear St Francis and ask if it is possible that I shall dare think differently from him or seek heaven any other way.
>
> I read too much of St F[rancis] de Sales so earnest for bringing all to the bosom of the Catholic church and I say to myself will I ever know better how to please God than [he] did and down I kneel to pour my tears to [him] and beg [him] to obtain faith for me.[95]

Elizabeth's 'dear Francis' continued to be a source of guidance after her conversion and when she embraced religious life. Her familiarity with Salesian spirituality was augmented when her community was placed under the supervision of the Sulpician fathers. Eventually, Father Simon Bruté was assigned as spiritual director to American-born Elizabeth, because his superior, also a Sulpician, said her soul was a great one but that a 'first class saint, a Saint Francis de Sales', would be needed to direct it.[96] Bruté recommended to Elizabeth many of de Sales' writings. Among the books from his own library that he lent her were Francis' *Letters*, a Circular Letter from the Visitation in Poland and the *Conferences*. The latter she translated in its entirety from the French original. Throughout the foundress' correspondence are references to de Sales and de Chantal drawn from her reading and from Bruté's direction. That the Sulpician saw Elizabeth Seton as another Jane de Chantal is clear. During her last retreat in 1820 taken under his direction, he continued to form her on the pattern of St Jane who, like Elizabeth, had been a wife, mother and foundress. Rereading the advice of Mother de Chantal to superiors, Mother Seton was to 'strive for the spirit of St Francis de Sales and Madame de Chantal, whose spirit was in fact that of her own community'.[97] During her last painful illness, it was the Savoyard bishop's words that gave meaning to her experience. 'We will have but the words of St Francis de Sales: "I have desired little – and I desire less than ever." '[98] It is worth noting that Mother Seton and her American Sulpician advisors seem to have emphasised those aspects of Salesian spirituality that were the most compatible with the austere spirit of the French School: to desire little, to abandon oneself to the grace of the moment, to adore the will of God, to strive for the perfect love of God through the gradual relinquishment of all loves but the love of God alone. These were the spiritual themes that they associated with the Salesian saints.

Mrs Seton was fluent in French and so could enjoy de Sales in the original, but many Americans were not familiar with the French tongue. This, however, did not inhibit the spread of Francis' popularity. An English version of the *Introduction to the Devout Life* was first published in America in 1706 and enjoyed a wide circulation. De Sales' influence was also enhanced by the dissemination of *The Garden of the Soul*, a prayer book compiled by English bishop Richard Challoner which included a condensed version of the ten introductory meditations from the *Introduction*, along with Salesian instructions on meditation.[99] Books like these provided the growing immigrant American Catholic populace with spiritual nurture.

> By 1848 over half a million children (mainly Catholic) were attending the national schools. As more and more people learned to read English, the new prayer books became the staple devotional diet of Irish homes. Indeed, the bundle that Paddy Leary took on his shoulder when he went off to Philadelphia almost certainly contained *The Garden of the Soul*.[100]

The close connection between the French or French-trained Catholic clergy and the fledgling Church in the new Republic meant that the names of Sts Francis de Sales and Jane de Chantal were well known and their Salesian spirit promoted. A seminal example is found in John Carroll (1735–1815), the first bishop in the newly formed United States. Carroll was from a notable and patriotic family: his brother Charles was present at the First Continental Congress, was elected to the Maryland legislature and served as a US senator. John, like many Catholics of the period, had been trained in Europe and joined the Jesuit Order. His training reflected the more humanistic strain of the French tradition represented especially by Francis de Sales as well as the British Catholic tradition and the Ignatian heritage. In the course of his studies Carroll had been introduced to the ideal of the Christian gentleman in the *Introduction to the Devout Life*. Salesian values of gentle persuasion, moderate asceticism and the centrality of charity in the spiritual life deeply impressed the future bishop and would form the basis of his own creative pastoral approach in the new world. Reflecting his Salesian sensibilities, Carroll's sermons were noted for their warmth and were expressions of his deeply interior piety which emphasised 'transforming into our hearts the sentiments and

affections of Jesus Christ.'[101] And, although the devotion to the
Sacred Heart by this time was no longer solely identified with
the Visitation Order, the practice of the devotion was promoted
by the United States' first Catholic bishop. In 1793, Carroll
ordered for pastoral dissemination 100 copies of *The Pious
Guide to Prayer and Devotion* compiled by the Jesuits of
Georgetown University (an institution that was closely associated with the Visitation convent in Georgetown). In part, the
Pious Guide was designed to refute the Jansenist criticism
that the devotion was crudely materialistic. It stressed
instead that the 'heart' was a symbol for the entire humanity
of Christ. In practising this devotion, it was claimed, the
Christian would model his or her heart on the divine original
and be gradually transformed. The goal of the Sacred Heart
devotion was to 'perform all our daily actions, in union with
the Sacred Heart; so that, when we pray, we pray with it;
when we love, we love with it; when we act, we act with and
in it; when we suffer we suffer in and for it'.[102] Francis de Sales
and Jane de Chantal themselves could not have expressed it
better.

The Visitation in America

Similar examples of the ubiquitous yet often hidden ways in
which the Salesian tradition informed the church in the New
World could be cited. But the practice of 'living Jesus' would
be more overtly expressed when the Order of the Visitation
was established on American soil. The first two groups of Catholic nuns to come to the United States were Carmelites, from
Antwerp, who established themselves at Port Tobacco, Maryland,[103] and three Poor Clares from France who initially settled
in Baltimore.[104] Bishop Carroll was acutely aware of the need
for educators in the new nation yet the Carmelites felt they
were called to continue their cloistered life, and the Poor
Clares were unsuccessful schoolmistresses as they had difficulty with the English language. Nevertheless, the French-
speaking women opened an Academy for young ladies in

Georgetown next to the college for men for which Bishop
Carroll and his successor Leonard Neale (1747–1817) had provided leadership. Neale, like Carroll, came from a prosperous
and influential family that generously served the nascent US
church. During his ministry in Philadelphia, Neale had come
into contact with three devout women who aspired to religious
life; one of them was Miss Alice Lalor. The three had met on
a ship sailing from Ireland to America and, sensing a union of
hearts, had purchased a dwelling in Philadelphia where they
prayed and lived together. A yellow fever epidemic broke up
the house and Miss Lalor's two companions died. For a time,
she returned to her home then, at Neale's suggestion, she
relocated to Georgetown with two new companions, a Mrs
Maria McDermott, and a Mrs Sharpe, both widows. Upon their
arrival these three seem to have co-operated with the Poor
Clares in running the school. Soon, the French religious
returned to their homeland, leaving the three 'Pious Ladies'
and those who later joined them as the Washington area
schoolmistresses destined to serve young women.

Convent tradition holds that during his early missionary
journeys, Neale had a vision of a great procession of religious
women in a habit unknown to him led by a woman of dignified
presence. Nearby a man, in his pontifical regalia, pronounced,
'You shall erect a house of this my order.' Apparently, years
later, when he was shown portraits of the Sts Francis de Sales
and Jane de Chantal, Neale recognised them as the man and
woman in his vision. But how much this vision gained meaning
in hindsight is a question. More verifiably, an early Neale
biographer reported:

> It was long a subject of serious meditation with him, and
> a point which occasioned him much embarrassment, to
> determine what particular institute to assign the ladies
> who had gradually joined the pious association. Their
> numbers had increased, their usefulness had become to
> be generally acknowledged and appreciated, but they had
> no rules of government, further than what emanated from

his pious direction, and what were of an unstable character. After long and mature deliberation aided by unceasing prayer to the Almighty, to direct his judgment in the selection of an order and discipline for their future conduct, the bishop determined to introduce the Institution of the Visitation, founded by St Francis de Sales, as best suited to the spirit of the age and the peculiar duties proposed for their secular occupation. The secular department of their duties they had all along practiced; it consisted mainly in the education of young females, and their proper instruction in religion and virtue.[105]

Incorporation into the Visitation was not all Neale's idea, however much hagiographical tradition might represent it as such. The Pious Ladies themselves were remarkably resourceful and self-generating, and the decision to seek formal acceptance into the Order was a shared decision.[106] Miss Lalor, and the Mmes Sharpe and McDermott were familiar with the Salesian spirit through their careful reading of the *Introduction to the Devout Life* and the *Spiritual Directory*. The Visitation was one of the most popular and influential orders in Europe – by 1773 more than 120 convents had been established in France alone – yet at the time the Pious Ladies aspired to be affiliated with the Order, political and religious chaos had descended on the French landscape. Communication across the Atlantic was difficult and for some time religious houses were suppressed. Many Visitation convents never reopened and it was 1822 before the 'Sainte Source' at Annecy was restored. Meanwhile, the American community gradually grew and the sisters, with their bishop, considered themselves Visitandines.[107] Resisting pressure to join forces with Elizabeth Seton's Sisters of Charity or with the Carmelites, in 1814 they took simple vows of their own. They as yet did not know the correct Visitation habit nor the necessary literature – custom books and such – with which to enter into a 'union of hearts' with their European sisters. Archbishop Neale's letters eventually reached the exiled Annecy community at Chambéry, and several other functioning houses sent forty of the distinctive Visitation crosses, the necessary books and a doll dressed in a miniature Visitation habit. In December of 1816 the first of the American women took solemn vows, sealing their incorporation into the Order with papal approval. Of necessity, some adaptation of the Rule had to be made for the different context of the New World, but the Pious Ladies, nurtured in the spirit of the *Introduction*, already knew what it was to 'live Jesus'. Neale wrote,

> Thus by the happy disposition of Divine Providence on the anniversary of the departure of St Francis de Sales from this life, existence and life were imparted to the first established community of his order in America.[108]

Situated adjacent to the developing nation's capital, the Visitation Monastery with its Academy was at the cross currents of American life and reflected all the critical movements and events of the next centuries. The first Pious Ladies, whose educational background was limited, were soon augmented by others who were trained teachers.[109] The archives of the first American Visitation contain fascinating documentation of the different women who joined the venture. A striking example is Mrs Jerusha Barber (Sr Mary Austin), who before her entry in 1817 had been a schoolmistress in an academy in New York where her husband was headmaster. When the Episcopalian couple converted to Catholicism, Mrs Barber's husband determined to enter the Jesuits and his wife joined the Visitation with their small daughters in tow. Her entry was a mixed blessing for the community. On the one hand, she was extremely well-educated and a superb teacher and quickly raised the levels of knowledge and skill of both pupils and instructors. On the other hand, her personal life was complex; when she first arrived there was some concern that she might be pregnant, then the question of what to do with her children arose. Despite all this, and the many other eventful occurrences that inevitably take place at the beginning of any venture, the school and monastery flourished.

The Academy began with two apostolates – to well-to-do boarders and to poor day-students from the surrounding area.[110] It opened its doors to Catholics and non-Catholics alike and over time became a prosperous and well-equipped institution. By 1828, under the spiritual guidance of Sulpician father Michael Wheeler, the boarding school was installing 'apparatus' for the teaching of the many branches of modern science. The young ladies also studied grammar, geography, arithmetic, composition, history, languages, music and painting as well as more practical subjects related to 'domestic economy' such as dressmaking, culinary arts, laundry and dairy inspection. As the years progressed the Academy curriculum evolved and continued to reflect the latest criteria of academic excellence. In the two centuries since its foundation the Georgetown Academy has educated generations of middle-class girls. In addition, it has numbered among its students the daughters of Washington's political, military, and literary élite, as well as the daughters and nieces of foreign ambassadors.[111] Academy alumnae are especially loyal to their *alma mater* because, for all the strictness of convent education, the Salesian spirit of gentle persuasion and 'winning hearts' has long pervaded the atmosphere.

From its American beginnings in sight of the Potomac River, the Order of the Visitation travelled west with the opening of the American frontier: foundations in Alabama, Illinois, Maryland, Missouri, Pennsylvania, Iowa, New York, Virginia, West Virginia, Minnesota, Kentucky, Idaho, Nebraska, Ohio, Washington and Georgia followed in the next century and a half.[112] All of these foundations carried the spirit of the founders with them. Because of the acute need for educators in the expanding territories, the Visitation in America became known primarily as a teaching order. Some academies became known for excellence in specific fields; an example is the Wheeling, West Virginia convent school that was noted for its music education. But, in other cases, local needs called communities to different ministries. Federal Way, Washington, Springfield, Missouri and Mobile, Alabama monasteries eventually turned to retreat ministry and sponsored retreat houses and programmes. On occasion, the work to which a monastery was called locally necessitated great change. The Dubuque, Iowa Visitation sisters had originally been asked by their local bishop to teach in the parish school across the street. When later canonical norms made this freedom of movement impossible, the nuns choose to leave the Order (but not renounce the Salesian spirit) to re-found in 1952 as a diocesan congregation so they could continue to teach in the parish school. Visitation schools were often one of the key community institutions that nurtured a growing American Catholic population during the nineteenth and early twentieth centuries. In the Midwest, the budding cities of St Paul and St Louis were served by Visitation academies that educated the daughters and future wives and mothers of the increasingly affluent and influential Catholic civic leaders. Indeed, prominent Catholic family surnames are found in the registers of both Visitation teachers and pupils throughout the United States. At the same time, in most academies, the sisters championed the education of girls who were not from the élite classes.

The active ministries of the American Visitation were never conceived as a substitute for the prayer that formed the core of the Order's charism. The contemplative dimension of Visitandine life was always paramount, whether expressed in the choir stall or in the classroom. At the turn of the twentieth century, during a time when the wider Church was re-emphasising the significance of the formal contemplative life, a number of well-to-do Catholics established endowments that allowed several existing Visitation communities to close their schools and focus exclusively on community contemplative practice. The monasteries of Wilmington, Delaware (Tyringham), Richmond, Virginia (Rockville), and Bethesda, Maryland followed this pattern. In the mid 1950s the question of institutional identity of the American Visitation was forced when, church-wide, contemplative orders were gathered together in federations for better mutual support. At this time, minor papal enclosure was established so that houses that had schools or other associated works could set aside part of the monastery property expressly for these works. In the United States two distinct federations of the Visitation Order were created. One group maintained schools. A second group engaged primarily in contemplative practice. At that time there were approximately twenty communities in existence. At the beginning of the twenty-first century, of the thirteen monasteries that are still in operation, seven operate schools or sponsor outreach to the surrounding community. Among these, the dissemination of Salesian spirituality among lay faculty, students, parents and alumni has become a priority. As it is no longer possible to simply imbibe the Salesian spirit from the sisters, who were once the majority of faculty and administration, innovative curricular initiatives and programmes have been developed that now carry the Salesian vision of a world of hearts into the neighbouring community.

The 'Nunz 'n the Hood'

Whether the Salesian world of hearts comes to life within the cloister, with its focus on the intimate union of human and divine, or whether the horizontal exchange of human heart to human heart is more visibly emphasised, the Visitation of Holy Mary is one of the principal bearers of the Salesian vision in the United States. Because Salesian spirituality is first a matter of the heart – Francis' dictum 'As the heart is the source of all our actions, as the heart is, so are they' is key here – it can be lived out in any number of differing ways. Even the Visitation itself is witness to this truth. Among the newest expressions of the Visitation charism is the monastery in Minneapolis, Minnesota. The foundation in 1989 had its genesis in the prayer of three Visitation sisters from the St Louis, Missouri community. All three had spent years as teachers at the Academy attached to the monastery which provided an exemplary education to an affluent population. All three had been deeply affected by the currents of Catholic social thought in the mid twentieth century, especially liberation theology with its hallmark emphasis on the 'option for the poor'. After consultations with varied people, the Second Federation of the Visitation provided funds for the three, and one other sister from the St Paul, Minnesota monastery, to live, pray and be among those who are marginalised in society. The choice of sites was telling: a large residence needing renovation in a tough, mainly African-American section of the city of Minneapolis.

For these women, who were soon dubbed the 'nunz 'n the hood', Salesian spirituality was a fitting preparation for creating an urban monastery. Salesian gentleness especially was a gift to the surrounding violence-plagued community. Aware that the very first Visitation had been organised with a flexible cloister – it had not been linked to any specific apostolic work but was a house that allowed women like Jane de Chantal to give themselves in attentive prayer to their beloved Jesus and then to 'Live Jesus!' in response to those in need in the neighbourhood – the Minneapolis sisters embarked on their journey. Through trial and error, the particular shape of their life gradually emerged, although the overarching canopy of their life is the Visitation rule. The traditional pattern of monastic prayer punctuates the day; an hour and a half of meditation and sacred reading and daily Mass are constants. The sisters are often joined in their tiny chapel in the house by visitors of all sorts; neighbours, priests or pastors, and fellow seekers desiring a place to pray. The needs of the surrounding community draw forth from them varied responses: providing afternoons of play and reading for neighbourhood children, forming a lay community, 'Visitation Neighbours', that serves among the poor and is nurtured in the Salesian vision, hosting a Hispanic parish young adult group, teaching piano and tutoring in mathematics, ministering to neighbours whose family members have been lost to urban violence, offering healing massage, networking with neighbourhood alliances concerned about affordable housing, or facilitating a Wise Women's group for the elders of the African-American community. At the heart of this monastic life in twenty-first century North America are the values of community, prayer and presence. Their mission statement echoes the Salesian vision of a world of hearts transformed from within and transforming the hearts around them.

It's not so much what we DO but who we ARE and who we BECOME through our involvement as Visitation sisters.

[We] express our contemplative way of life by living, praying and ministering to those who are often disregarded in our world today. We came to North Minneapolis to discover, through a relationship with the people of our 'hood', the Christ active in our city.[113]

In whatever particular form it takes, the American Visitation continues to 'Live Jesus!' in ways that mirror the original vision of Francis de Sales and Jane de Chantal: the vision of a world of hearts speaking to hearts.

Centered where Jesus gave us his Spirit, our life becomes a way of love, of action and surrender, of wholeheartedness and detachment. Our living is characterized by attentiveness to the will of God and to our liberty of spirit. Therefore, our life is a life of prayer – continuous prayer, simple prayer – a being at home, at rest in the heart of Jesus, learning and expressing his inmost desire that we ourselves may become faithful expressions of God's will.

We are called to the practice of love rather than to austerity. Two virtues in particular form the warp through which the woof of love is woven. These are humility and gentleness: a humility consecrated in truth, the humility of Mary's 'Magnificat'; and a gentleness commissioned to lay life down, the gentleness of the heart of Jesus.

Our life, our only life, is that life of love incarnated by Jesus, proclaimed by the church, and meant to be shared that all might live. We share this abundant life primarily in prayer, a prayer that is lived in community.

Our model for this life in community is Mary who pondered, but who also went as she pondered, went to the rhythm of Jesus' heart. We believe that each day she continues to make her loving visitation inviting us to 'Live Jesus' in the church and in the world.[114]

7. THE UNIVERSAL CALL TO HOLINESS: THE SECOND VATICAN COUNCIL AND THE SALESIAN SAINTS

The saints transcend their own times because they live for and in God . . . their history is carried in the Church's history like a gulf-stream that surges toward the ocean. They are present among us, whether we are aware of it or not. This seems to be particularly true of Saint Francis de Sales. Even if the context of his life was quite different from ours one would have a difficult time concluding from this that he has lost his relevance for us today . . . If one wished to disclose the imprint of Saint Francis de Sales on the contemporary church it would not be difficult to discover, if not his name, at least his perceptible influence in between the lines of many of the great texts of the [Second Vatican] Council . . . On the occasion of his fourth centenary it seems fitting to recognize the debt of gratitude that our generation owes to him. For us he is near, living and real. His warm, luminous and serene presence helps us to understand and live the anticipated joy of the communion of saints.[1]

Léon Joseph Cardinal Suenens

Commenting in the mid twentieth century on the ubiquitous influence Francis de Sales has had on French spirituality, historian Pierre Serouet remarked, 'no one would ever dream of trying to give an accounting of an influence that was at the same time so clear and so diffuse'. Serouet continued by citing the earlier opinion of literary historian Henri Bremond who claimed that the Savoyard's influence was so great that Catholic spirituality was in fact indistinguishable from Salesian spirituality.[2] Given the present-day geographical reach of Catholicism and the rich variety of spiritual traditions that flourish, these comments today seem overstated. Nonetheless, they point to a truth about the Salesian heritage: that through many different channels, the vision of a world of human and divine hearts first crafted at the dawn of the seventeenth century was communicated to and embraced by a remarkable number of Christians over the course of four centuries. That vision, or essential aspects of that vision, is in fact refracted in the documents of the Second Vatican Council.

Cardinal Suenens, himself one of the chief architects of the Council, credited Francis with an influence that could be perceived between the lines of the great conciliar texts.[3] In Suenens' eyes, Chapter V of *Lumen Gentium* (the *Dogmatic Constitution on the Church*) echoed the thought of the Savoyard saint. That fifth chapter, entitled the 'Universal Call to Holiness', stressed that the same call is issued to cleric and lay alike by virtue of their baptism. This sense that the Church itself, and all members in it according to their differing 'states in life', are called to 'be perfect as your Father is perfect' is indeed at the centre of the Salesian world of hearts. Beyond this, Suenens saw Francis' influence in *Gaudium et Spes* (*Constitution on the Church in the Modern World*) in the chapter on marriage. 'It seems commonplace today to consider love to be at the heart of marriage and to accent the necessary interpersonal communion of spouses . . . [however] those who have worked on the elaboration of these texts know that . . . it took some tenacity to introduce this [idea] and to hold to it in the face of a purely juridical notion of marriage.'[4] That Francis de Sales placed love at the centre of all human relationships is true, and his ever-popular *Introduction to the Devout Life* has kept that understanding before generations of married people. Finally, the Cardinal considered Vatican II to in some sense mark the posthumous triumph of Francis de Sales' flexible vision of women's communities. Suenens saw in his original plan for the Visitation an inspired premonition of the future of religious life.

A somewhat more nuanced evaluation of Francis de Sales' imprint on the mid twentieth century church has been offered by Dominican theologian Yves Congar. While appreciating Francis' emphasis on the laity, Congar points out that the Savoyard was not a complete innovator in this regard. Several centuries of gradual awakening of lay participation and spiritual vitality preceded the *Introduction*. Francis' efforts he deemed 'a simple acceleration of an already long-awakened and living movement'.[5] In similar fashion, Congar evaluated Francis as a saint for the contemporary age of ecumenism. Ages differ, and 'ecumenism is something other than mission work and is motivated by something other than proselytism'. Yet while situating Francis in historical context, the Dominican saw in him a forerunner of the trends that characterise the contemporary Catholic Church. And appropriately, and insightfully, he cut to the heart of Salesian spirituality when he answered his own questions:

> What would be the thoughts of Francis de Sales today? What sermon would he give if invited to preach during the Week of Universal Prayer for Unity? What statement would he bring from Geneva and from the Chablais to the Council of John XXIII? We can be sure of one thing: they would be thoughts and words dictated by his charity and his sole desire of following the indications of the will of God.[6]

In paring down Francis de Sales' vision to these essentials, Congar shows himself to be an accurate interpreter of the Salesian spirit. Love, for the Savoyard, and for the spiritual tradition he fathered, is the beginning, end and means of the entire Christian life. Steeped in a sense of a loving God's merciful and providential care for creation and in a trust in the goodness and capacity of human beings to love, the Salesian world is envisioned as a world of hearts. Human hearts are drawn to intimacy with the Heart of God and with one another through the Heart of Christ. Human hearts beat in rhythm with the heartbeat of God as they 'Live Jesus', and allow the Heart of the gentle, humble Saviour to inhabit and animate them. Human hearts rest in the Heart of God like children in the arms of a parent or lovers on the breast of a beloved. Human hearts beat and breathe together in friendship, in families, in intentional communities, in the Church and in loving service, revealing the Heart of the gentle Jesus alive in the world. Salesian spirituality is, then, essentially a matter of the heart and can be lived out in myriad ways. Although several devotional practices are associated with the tradition, such as the observance of First Fridays or consecration to the Sacred Heart, it is not primarily characterised by a particular lifestyle or set of practices, but with a quality of heart that is expressed in word and deed. With the freedom of the child of God, the Salesian responds to the God of Love both by active engagement with God's 'signified will' and by surrender to the will of God's 'good pleasure'. With the freedom of a lover of God, a follower of the Salesian way has a heart nestled near the Heart of God and a gentle heart open to others in whatever way Love and circumstances call forth.

Over the centuries, the vision of a world of hearts has been experienced and expressed in a variety of social, political, ecclesial and theological contexts. Visitandine Margaret Mary Alacoque's revelations of the Heart of Jesus that set the pattern for the officially sanctioned cult of the Sacred Heart reflected the somber Augustinian theological perspective of her era, one that differed from the more optimistic devout humanism of Francis de Sales.[7] In nineteenth-century Paris, Monsiegneur de Ségur saw the conversion of Protestants as a primary goal of his Association of Francis de Sales, while amid the violence of inner-city Minneapolis in the twenty-first century, the Visitation 'nunz 'n the hood' see themselves as cultivating the non-violent Heart of Christ in their ministry equally to persons of all faith traditions. The families of Don Bosco Salesians highlight the method of 'preventive pedagogy' in their work with marginalised youth, while many of the

Oblate Fathers and Brothers and Oblate Sisters in their varied apostolates emphasise the practice of the *Spiritual Directory*. A housewife taking a retreat with the *Introduction to the Devout Life* might gather a 'spiritual nosegay' at the end of the day to inhale the sweet perfume of prayer, while a cloistered Visitandine might identify with Jane de Chantal's interior experience of the 'martyrdom of love'. These differing expressions of the Salesian world of hearts nonetheless are intimately and essentially one. The master metaphors of the tradition continue to be refracted over and over again across the centuries.

THE SALESIAN SAINTS

The official Roman Catholic process of saint-making is a complex and often contested one.[8] Despite this, it is a not insignificant fact that so many of the members of the Salesian spiritual family have been formally acknowledged by the ecclesial community to which they belong as both models of the Christian life and intercessors on whom the faithful might depend. They are publicly acknowledged as somehow both close to God and close to the human heart.

Counted among those who have been declared 'Saint' are, of course, Francis de Sales and Jane de Chantal. The Visitation Order counts among its canonised forebears not only its mother-foundress but also Margaret Mary Alacoque. Of the principles of the nineteenth-century Salesian Pentecost, John Bosco, Léonie Aviat, foundress of the Oblate Sisters of St Francis de Sales, and Maria Domenica Mazzarello, foundress of Daughters of Mary Help of Christians, have been canonised, as has Dominic Savio, one of Don Bosco's early young followers. Scores of other members of the Salesian spiritual family, including seven Visitandines of Spain martyred during the Spanish Civil War,[9] can claim the official titles of Blessed or Venerable.[10] Of what possible interest is this here, in this survey of Salesian spirituality? Very little unless one takes seriously the fundamental principal of the Salesian vision:

that human hearts are created to love deeply and fully, to experience the depth of divine desire, and to love as they have first been loved. Holiness, sanctity, sainthood: in the Salesian lexicon these words do not refer to an élite cadre of super-human heroes or to a chilly, inhuman piety; they are not reserved for religious professionals or for individuals who are 'not of this world'. Holiness is the destiny of all human beings. Sanctity is simply the deep realisation of the life given over to Love. The saints are all those who give their hearts to Love's promptings. And all are created for and invited into the mystery of the divine and human world where heart speaks gently to heart.

Doctor of Divine Love, Francis de Sales would not rest until the faithful had welcomed God's love in order to live fully, turned their hearts to God and united with Him. It is thus that, under his guidance, any number of Christians have walked in the way of holiness; he showed them that all are called to an intense spiritual life, no matter what their profession or circumstances because [as he taught] 'the church is an infinitely variegated garden of flowers, there are therefore diverse heights, colors, scents, in sum, different perfections. While each has its own value, gracefulness and brilliance, all together in their variety they are stunningly beautiful.' A good and gentle man, who knew how to express the mercy and patience of God to all whom he met, he proposed an exacting but serene spirituality founded on love because 'this is the greatest happiness in this life and in eternity'.

Pope John Paul II, 2002
Letter to the Bishop of Annecy
on the Occasion of the Fourth Centenary
of Francis de Sales' Episcopal Ordination[11]

NOTES

Chapter 1: The Salesian Spiritual Tradition

1. *Bérulle and the French School: Selected Writings*, edited by William M. Thompson, translated by Lowell M. Glendon, SS (New York/Mahwah: Paulist Press, 1989), p. 80.
2. Francis de Sales and Jane de Chantal are sometimes seen as progenitors of the French School. Pierre de Bérulle, the early shaper of that early tradition, and de Sales were part of the spiritual renaissance at the dawn of the seventeenth century and knew one another. Figures of the later French School such as John Eudes, and Jean Jacques Olier admired and drew upon their Salesian predecessors. Yet the two traditions remain quite distinct in some of their fundamental assumptions. See Wendy M. Wright, 'The Salesian and Bérullean Spiritual Traditions', *Alive for God Now: Proceedings from the Conference Exploring Contemporary Influences from the French School* (Buffalo: St John Eudes Center, 1995), pp. 157–67.
3. On Jane's contributions see the Introduction by Wendy M. Wright and Joseph F. Power, OSFS to *Francis de Sales, Jane de Chantal: Letters of Spiritual Direction*, trans. Péronne-Marie Thibert, VHM (Mahwah, NJ: Paulist Press, 1988), pp. 70–86.
4. Henri L'Honoré, 'Ramifications de la famille Salésienne,' in *L'Unidivers Salésien: Saint François de Sales hier et aujourd'hui*, textes réunis et publiés par Hélène Bordes et Jacques Hennequin (Paris: Université de Metz, 1994), pp. 459–71.

Chapter 2: A World of Hearts: Francis de Sales

1. *Oeuvres de Saint François de Sales*, edition complète d'après les autographes et les editions originales par les soins des Religieuses de la Visitation du Premier Monastère d' Annecy, 26 vols (Annecy: Nierat, 1892–1964), V, *Traité de l'amour de Dieu*, 9. This is the critical edition of Francis de Sales' work. The complete multi-volumed set includes: Vol. 1: *Les Controverses*, 2: *Défense de l'Estendart de la Sainte Croix*, 3: *Introduction à la Vie Dévote*, 4 and 5:

Traité de l'Amour de Dieu, 6: *Les Vrays Entretiens Spirituels*, 7–10: *Sermons*, 11–21: *Lettres*, 22–26: *Opuscules*.

2. *St Francis de Sales: A Testimony by St Chantal*, trans. Elisabeth Stopp, (Hyattsville, Maryland: Institute of Salesian Studies, 1967), pp. 138–9.

3. Among the most presently accessible and readable biographies in English are André Ravier, SJ, *Francis de Sales: Sage and Saint*, trans. Joseph D. Bowler, (San Francisco: Ignatius Press, 1988); Dirk Koster, OSFS, *Francis de Sales*, trans. from the Dutch (The Netherlands: Bert Post, 2000); Michael de la Bedoyere, *Saint Maker* (Manchester, New Hampshire: Sophia Institute Press, 1998), originally published as *François de Sales* (New York: Harper Bros., 1960); and E. J. Lajeunie, OP, *Saint Francis de Sales: The Man, the Thinker, His Influence*, trans. Rory O'Sullivan, OSFS, 2 Vols. (Bangalore, India: SFS Publications, 1986). See also the illuminating collection of essays by Elisabeth Stopp, *A Man to Heal Differences: Essays and Talks on St Francis de Sales* (Philadelphia: Saint Joseph's University Press, 1997). On English language works on the Salesian tradition see the web-based bibliography by Fr Joseph Boenzi, SDB, 'Saint Francis de Sales: Toward a Complete Bibliography of English-language Works.' http://www4.desales.edu/~salesian/fdsbibli.html

4. The culture of Savoy was influenced by both France and Italy but retained its own distinctiveness. The House of Savoy, a major player in the politics of Christendom, reigned for over one thousand years. See *Histoire de la Savoie*, ed. Paul Guichonnet (Toulouse: Eduard Privat, 1973). I am indebted to Dr Patricia Siegel and to Fr Joseph Boenzi for their research on the history of Savoy.

5. John W. O'Malley has coined the term Early Modern Catholicism. Cf. *Early Modern Catholicism: Essays in Honor of John W. O'Malley, SJ*, ed. Kathleen Comerford and Hilmar M. Pabel (Toronto: University of Toronto Press, 2001).

6. The definitive treatment of early Jesuit education is found in John W. O'Malley, *The First Jesuits* (Cambridge, MA: Harvard University Press, 1993).

7. For a thorough discussion of the saint and the Song of Songs see André Brix, OSFS, *François de Sales: Commente le Cantique des Cantiques*, (France: n.p., n.d.). See also *St Francis de Sales: The Mystical Exposition of the Canticle of Canticles*, trans. Thomas F. Dailey, OSFS (Center Valley, PA: Allentown College of St Francis de Sales, 1996).

8. Ravier. *Francis de Sales: Sage and Saint*, p. 32.

9. Cf. William B. Marceau, CSB, *Optimism in the Works of St Francis de Sales* (Bangalore, India: SFS Publications, 1983).

10. *St Francis de Sales, Selected Letters*, trans. Elisabeth Stopp (New York: Harper and Bros., 1960), pp. 261–2.

11. In this de Sales sided with the 'Molinist camp' (from the name of the Jesuit Molina who advanced the issue) in a heated debate that rocked the Church at the time.

12. See *Spiritual Exercises by St Francis de Sales*, trans. William N. Doughtery, osfs, ed. Joseph F. Chorpenning, osfs (Toronto: Peregrina Publishing, 1993).

13. Ibid., p. 30.

14. Ibid., p. 35.

15. Francis' practice of the sacred sleep has its origins in the monastic practice of *lectio divina* (spiritual reading) in which scripture or other edifying material is deeply assimilated through a process of *lectio* (reading), *meditatio* (meditation), *oratio* (prayer), and *contemplatio* (contemplation).

16. *St Francis de Sales: A Testimony by St Chantal*, p. 168.

17. Cf. *Religious Orders of the Catholic Reformation: Essays In Honor of John C. Olin on His Seventy-fifth Birthday*, ed. Richard L. De Molen (New York: Fordham University Press, 1994).

18. On the mission to the Chablais see Patricia J. Siegel, 'The Unsung Hero of the Reformation: Saint Francis de Sales', *War and Its Uses: Conflict and Creativity*, eds. Jürgen Kleist and Bruce A. Butterfield (New York: Peter Lang, 1999), pp. 47–59 and R. Balducelli, 'Saint Francis de Sales on Tradition: a Discussion of *Les Controverses* II, 2, 1–2', *Salesian Studies* 2:1 (October 1963), pp. 17–28 and Midathada Mariadas, *The Missionary Spirit of St Francis de Sales, Apostle of the Chablais* (Bangalore: SFS Publications, 1990).

19. Henri Brémond coined the term. See his *A Literary History of Religious Thought in France: from the Wars of Religion Down to Our Own Time*, Vol. 1, *Devout Humanism* (London: Society for Promoting Christian Knowledge, 1930). Not all scholars agree with his definition and his characterisation of Francis' brand of humanism.

20. Francis de Sales, *Introduction to the Devout Life*, Pt. I., Chap 1, trans. Missionaries of St Francis de Sales (Bangalore, India: SFS Publications, 1990), p. 11.

21. *Oeuvres*, V, *Traité*, pp. 203–208. On the Salesian world of hearts see Wendy M. Wright, ' "That Is What It is Made For": The Image of the Heart in the Spirituality of Francis de Sales and Jane de Chantal', *Spiritualities of the Heart*, ed. Annice Callahan, rscj (Mahwah, NJ: Paulist Press, 1990), pp. 143–58 and John Abbruzze, *The Theology of the Heart in the Writings of St Francis de Sales* (Rome: Pontifical University of St Thomas Aquinas, 1983).

22. Jane de Chantal quotes him posthumously at the proceedings for his canonisation. See *St Francis de Sales: A Testimony by St Chantal*, p. 64.

23. *Oeuvres*, III, *Introduction*, pp. 216–17.

24. *On the Preacher and Preaching by St Francis de Sales*, trans. John K. Ryan (US: Henry Regnery Co., 1964), p. 64.

25. *Oeuvres*, XII, *Lettres* pp. 2, 285.
26. Terence A. McGoldrick, *The Sweet and Gentle Struggle: Francis de Sales on the Necessity of Spiritual Friendship* (Lanham: University Press of America, 1996), pp. 2–68 and René Champagne, *François de Sales ou la passion de l'autre* (Montreal: Mediaspaul, 1998). In his *Introduction* de Sales distinguishes between spiritual friendship and other types of friendships including frivolous flirtations.
27. The 'Universal Call to Holiness' is articulated in *Lumen Gentium*, the *Dogmatic Constitution on the Church*. See Yves M. J. Congar, OP, 'Francis de Sales Today,' *Salesian Studies*, 3 (Winter 1966), 5–9; Léon Joseph Cardinal Suenens, 'Saint François de Sales et Vatican II' in *Saint François de Sales, Témoignages et Mélanges*, Mémoires et Documents publiés par L'Académie Salésienne, Tome LXXX (Amabilly-Annemasse: Editions Franco-Swisses, 1968), pp. 23–4. Germane here too is the allocution *Sabaudiae gemma* of Pope Paul VI, 29 January 1967, which states 'No one in the recent Doctors of the Church more than St Francis de Sales anticipated the deliberations and decisions of the Second Vatican Council with such a keen and progressive insight. He renders his contribution by the example of his life, by the wealth of his true and sound doctrine, by the fact that he has opened and strengthened the spiritual ways of Christian perfection for all states and conditions of life.' I am also indebted to Fr Power for his unpublished research on Salesian spirituality in Vatican I and II.
28. Quoted in Ravier, *Francis de Sales: Sage and Saint*, p. 131.
29. The completed version of the *Treatise* was more overtly inspired by Jane de Chantal and the Sisters of the Visitation community.
30. Ravier, *Francis de Sales: Sage and Saint*, p. 25.
31. The sermons, in fact, do not translate particularly well for devotional readers, although they are treasure chests of riches for scholars. For most of his life the bishop spoke from notes and his sermons were transcribed by listeners. Much is lost in such a process, especially tone, nuance, the felicitous turn of phrase, gesture, facial expression, and such. In short, the medium *was* the message in de Sales' case. Consult Hélène Bordes' lifetime scholarly accomplishment, *Les sermons de François de Sales*, Doctorat d'etat, 1989, (France: Université de Metz). See also her summary of the thesis, 'The Sermons of St Francis de Sales', in *Salesian Insights*, ed. William C. Marceau, CSB (Bangalore, India: Indian Institute of Spirituality, 1999), pp. 130–43. For English translations of some of the sermons see *The Sermons of St Francis de Sales*, ed. Lewis S. Fiorelli, OSFS, trans. Nuns of the Visitation (Rockford, IL: Tan Books, 1985–87). I. *On Prayer*. II. *On Our Lady*. III. *On Lent*. IV. *For Advent and Christmas*. See too Francis de Sales, *Sermons on Saint Joseph*, trans. ed. Joseph F. Chorpenning, OSFS (Toronto: Peregrina Publishing, 2000).
32. See *Oeuvres*, V for *Traité de l'amour de Dieu*. There is also a newer

edition with critical introduction by André Ravier, SJ, *Saint François de Sales, Oeuvres*, Bibliothèque de la Pléiade (Paris: Éditions Gallimard, 1969). A readable and accessible English translation is Francis de Sales, *The Love of God*, trans. Vincent Kerns, MSFS (Westminster, MD: The Newman Press, 1962). A more recent readable translation is Francis de Sales, *Introduction to the Devout Life*, trans. Armind Nazareth, OSFS, Antony Mookenthottam, OSFS, Antony Kolencherry, OSFS (Bangalore, India: SFS Publications., 1990).

33. Insight into this unique teaching is found in Joseph F. Power, OSFS, 'Entre l'une et l'autre volonté divine', in *L'Unidivers Salésien: Saint François de Sales hièr et aujourd' hui*, textes réunis et publiées par Hélène Bordes et Jacques Hennequin (Paris: Université de Metz, 1994), pp. 265–76.

34. *Treatise*, Book 9.

35. For another view see Ravier's introduction to the *Treatise* in the Pléiade edition of the *Oeuvres*, 323. The chapters in the *Treatise* that deal with the exercises of love and union with God in prayer are said to have been influenced by, indeed written for, Francis' friend Jane de Chantal and the early members of the Visitation.

36. Dirk Koster's biography provides a fresh view on the subject of these failures.

Chapter 3: *La Sainte Source*:
Jane de Chantal and the Visitation of Holy Mary

1. *Jeanne Françoise Frémyot de Chantal, Sa Vie et ses oeuvres,* Éditions authentique publiée par les soins des Religieuses du Monastère de la Visitation Sainte Marie d'Annecy (Paris: Plon, 1874), IV, *Lettres* pp. 1, 290–91. The complete works is eight volumes: Vol. 1: *Mémoire sur la vie et les vertus de Sainte Jeanne-Françoise Frémyot de Chantal. Par la Mère Françoise-Madeleine de Chaugy*. 2 and 3: *Oeuvres diverses*. 4–8: *Lettres*. See also Jeanne de Chantal, *Correspondance*, Edition critique, établie et annotée par Soeur Marie-Patricia Burns, VHM, Five tomes (Alençon: Les Editions du Cerf Centre d'études Franco-Italien des Universités de Turin et de Savoie, 1986–1993), Vol. 1, pp. 516 and 451. This newer and most important critical edition of the letters divides this undated missive into two fragments.

2. The best biography of Jane in English is Elisabeth Stopp's *Madame de Chantal: Portrait of a Saint* (Westminster, MD: The Newman Press, 1963; reprint, Stella Niagara, NY: De Sales Resource Center, 2002).

3. *Francis de Sales, Jane de Chantal: Letters of Spiritual Direction*, pp. 123–5.

4. Quoted in Wendy M. Wright, *Bond of Perfection: Jeanne de Chantal*

and François de Sales (Mahwah, NJ: Paulist Press, 1983; reprint, Stella Niagara, NY: De Sales Resource Center, 2001), p. 77.

5. This interpretation was given by Françoise-Madeleine de Chaugy, Jane's great niece and secretary, whose memories give us our most detailed and intimate glimpse into the Baroness' life and spirit.

6. On their friendship, see *Bond of Perfection* and McGoldrick, *The Sweet and Gentle Struggle*.

7. *Oeuvres*, XII, *Lettres* pp. 2, 354.

8. *Oeuvres*, XIII, *Lettres* pp. 3, 147; *Bond of Perfection*, p. 123.

9. Ibid., p. 295; *Bond of Perfection*, p. 124.

10. Stopp, *Madame de Chantal*, p. 137–8.

11. Jane is frequently remembered primarily as the saint who stepped over the body of her son as she left the world to enter religious life. Celse-Bénigne did indeed throw himself across the doorstep at the time of her leave taking. But even if his father had lived and his mother remained, he would have gone to live with his uncle to receive an education. Jane was devastated by her son's theatrical display, having carefully prepared everyone for the upcoming transition. The congregation she was joining made allowance for him to visit and for her to leave to care for family business. Years later after she had arranged a felicitous match for him he wrote to his mother that had she remained in the world she could not have cared for or provided for him any better than she in fact did.

12. On the Visitation, see *Visitation et Visitandines aux XVII^eet XVIIIe siècles* (Actes du Colloque d'Annecy, 1999), Études réunites et presentées par Bernard Dompnier et Dominique Julia, C.E.R.C.O.R., Travaux et Recherches XIV (Saint-Étienne: Publications de l'Université de Saint-Étienne; 2001). Also see Marie-Ange Duvignacq-Glessgen, *L'Ordre de la Visitation à Paris aux XVIIe et XVIIIe siècles* (Paris: Éditions du Cerf, 1994) and Gabriel Joppin, SJ, *La Visitation Sainte-Marie* (Casterman/Paris/Tournai: Éditions Salvator – Mulhouse, 1967). A critical source for the continuing history of the Visitation is *Année Sainte des Religieuses de la Visitation Sainte-Marie*, 12 Vol. (Annecy: Burdet, 1867–1871).

13. Scholarship has long perpetrated the idea that the Visitation was originally intended to be an active community and that, when it was formally enclosed in 1618, the bishop's dream was frustrated. Often scholars point to the Daughters of Charity founded by Vincent de Paul and Louise de Marillac in 1633 as the realisation of Francis' dream. The reality of the origins is more subtle than that. While the Visitandines originally took no formal vows nor observed a formal cloister, they were not created to do a particular work beyond the 'work' of living Jesus. Theirs was primarily a life of prayer with outreach as necessitated by the needs of their neighbours. See Wendy M. Wright, 'The Visitation of Holy Mary: The First Years (1610–1618)' in *Essays on the Religious Orders of the Catholic Refor-*

mation, ed. Richard De Molen (New York: Fordham University, 1994), pp. 217–240.

14. Wright, *Bond of Perfection*, pp. 140–41.
15. Jane's own mother had died giving birth when Jane was only eighteen months old. Jane grew up with a sense of the motherly protection of the Virgin Mary.
16. I am indebted here to all members of the 1998 Salesian seminar but especially to Joseph F. Chorpenning, OSFS and Dr Hélène Bordes. See his 'Connecting Mysteries: The Visitation and the Holy Family in the Salesian Tradition (from St Francis de Sales to the *Année Sainte* [1867–1871])' in *La Sagrada Familia en el siglo XIX*: Actas del Cuarto Congreso Internacional sobre La Sagrada Familia (Barcelona: Hijos de la Sagrada Familia/Nazarenum, 1999), pp. 811–33; and his ' "Mother of our Savior and Cooperator in Our Salvation": *Imitatio Mariae* and the Biblical Mystery of the Visitation in Francis de Sales', *Marian Studies* 53 (2002). See too Hélène Bordes, 'Charité et humilité dans l'oeuvre de François de Sales', *XVII siècle*, 43 (1991), pp. 15–25, and her 'La méditation du mystère de la Visitation par François de Sales et l'esprit de l'ordre de la Visitation', in *Visitation et Visitandines*, pp. 69–88.
17. For the Incarnation as kiss, see *The Sermons of St Francis de Sales on Our Lady*, pp. 135–6.
18. Bordes, 'Méditation du Mystère de la Visitation', p. 71.
19. *Sermons . . . On Our Lady*, p. 52.
20. *Sermons . . . On Our Lady*, p. 159.
21. See Chorpenning, 'Connecting Mysteries', on this. The Holy Family devotion and cult of St Joseph were coming into their own at the crest of the seventeenth century. Artists often depicted the 'double visitation' of Mary and Joseph to Elizabeth and Zechariah. De Sales blends together the mystery of the Visitation and that of the Holy Family to illuminate his relational spiritual vision. See also Chorpenning's monograph, *The Holy Family Devotion: A Brief History*, Lumière sur la Montagne 8 (Montréal: Centre de Recherche et de documentation Oratoire Saint-Joseph, 1997) which also contains an extended commentary on St Francis' views on the subject.
22. Francis de Sales' method of biblical interpretation was traditional. He assumed that there were literal, allegorical, moral and mystical meanings to be drawn from the inspired word. On his method see, *On the Preacher and Preaching*.
23. *Douceur* is often translated in English as meekness, suavity or sweetness. None of these do the term justice.
24. *Sa vie et ses oeuvres*, XVII, 26: Letter MCCXXIII to Mère de Bréchard. Also in *Sainte Jeanne de Chantal: Correspondance*, édition critique, Tome II, 353 (Lettre 658).
25. See Marie-Patricia Burns, 'La tendresse en Ste. Jeanne de Chantal', in *Annales Salesiennes*, 3 (1972), 10–11. On Jane's maternal style,

also see Wendy M. Wright, 'La douceur maternelle dans la direction spirituelle de Jeanne de Chantal', in *L'Unidivers Salésien*, pp. 307–319, and Isabelle Brian, 'La Lettre et l'espirit: Jeanne de Chantal, directrice spirituelle', in *Visitation et Visitandines*, pp. 53–67.

26. *Sa vie et ses oeuvres*, VII, 557, Lettre MDCCCLXXII. This updated letter is found in v. 6, pp. 620–22, in the Cerf. edition of Jane's letters edited by M. P. Burns.

27. Wendy M. Wright, 'Jane de Chantal's Guidance of Women: The Community of the Visitation and Womanly Values', in *Modern Christian Spirituality: Methodological and Historical Essays*, ed. Bradley C. Hanson (Atlanta, Georgia: Scholar's Press, 1990), pp. 113–38.

28. Ibid.

29. For an illuminating discussion of the spirituality of the Visitation in the century and a half after Jane's death, see the chapter based on the Circular Letters that passed between convents, 'Regard à l'intérieure d'une congrégation féminine', in Jean Delumeau, *Un chemin d'histoire: Chrétienneté et christianisation* (France: Fayard, Librarie Arthème, 1981), pp. 209–30.

30. Roger Dévos, 'Le testament spirituel de Sainte Jeanne-Françoise de Chantal et l'affaire du visiteur apostolique', in *Revue d'Histoire de la Spiritualité*, 48 (1972), pp. 453–76, and 49 (1973), pp. 199–226, 341–66.

31. Wright, *Bond of Perfection*, p. 160.

32. *Sa vie et ses oeuvres*, pp. 6, 114.

33. Ibid., II, p. 324.

34. Ibid., I, p. 341. Volume I, the *Mémoire* was written by Françoise-Madeleine de Chaugy, Jane's secretary.

35. *Responses de nostre très honorée et digne Mère Jeanne Françoise Frémyot de Chantal sur les règles, constitutions et coustumier de nostre ordre de la Visitation* (Paris, 1632), pp. 517–24.

36. Elisabeth Stopp writes of Jane's distinctive spirit in *Hidden in God: Essays and Talks on St Jane Frances de Chantal* (Philadelphia: Saint Joseph's University Press, 1999), esp. pp. 71–82, 93–108, and 109–116. See also Wendy M. Wright, 'Jeanne de Chantal and the "Martyrdom of Love": the Exploration of a Theme' in *Salesian Insights*, ed. Marceau, pp. 13–28.

37. *Sa vie et ses oeuvres*, I, *Mémoire*, pp. 41–42.

38. Ibid., p. 212. In modern versions, the Psalm is numbered 27.

39. Ibid., p. 214.

40. Ibid., p. 215.

41. Ibid., pp. 356–57. Chaugy emphasises the themes of abandonment and suffering when she writes her memoir of Jane. This interpretation of Jane's experience has been unquestioned. Suffice it to say that from other examples of Jane's writing – her letters, her recorded

Réponses, talks on the Constitutions and customs – this same emphasis shines through.

42. Marie-Patricia Burns, VHM, *Françoise-Madeleine de Chaugy: dans l'ombre et la lumière de la canonisation de François de Sales* (Annecy: Académie Salésienne, 2002), pp. 35–6.

43. On the new orders see *Essays on the Religious Orders of the Catholic Reformation*, pp. 216–50.

Chapter 4: 'A Great Light':
Diffusion of the Salesian Spirit

1. Quoted in Raymond Darricau, 'Saint François de Sales d'après l'oeuvre du Père Nicolas Caussin, Jesuite (1583–1651)', in *L'Unidivers Salésien*, p. 348.

2. Four *Lives* were composed immediately after Francis' death. By Goulu, by Messure de Longueterre, an ecclesiastic belonging to the bishop's Annecy entourage, by Franciscan Minim Louis de la Rivère, and by Philibert de Bonneville, a Savoyard Capuchin. All were acquaintances of Francis and worked in collaboration with de Sales' brothers, Jean and Louis, as well as with Jane de Chantal. Of the four, Goulu's is the one with merit. See Elisabeth Stopp, 'Jean Goulu and his "Life" of Saint Francis de Sales', *Modern Language Review*, 62 (1967), 226–37. Goulu asked Jane for her written impressions of the deceased which she supplied. See also Elisabeth Stopp, 'A Character Sketch of St Francis de Sales: St Chantal's Letter of December 1623 to Dom Jean de Saint-François,', *Salesian Studies*, 3–4 (1966–67), pp. 44–55.

3. See Darricau, 'Saint François de Sales d'après l'oeuvre du Père Nicolas Caussin'. Caussin's intent was not to write a life of the bishop but to present him as a model of the spiritual life and of spiritual directors.

4. Jean-Pierre Camus, *The Spirit of Francis de Sales, Bishop and Prince of Geneva*, translated by Henrietta Louise Farrer Lear, new impression ed. (London: Longmans, Green, 1921); *The Spirit of St François de Sales*, edited and newly translated, and with an introduction by Carl Franklin Kelley (New York: Harper, 1952); *The Spirit of St François de Sales*, edited and newly translated, and with an introduction by Carl Franklin Kelley (London, Longmans, 1953). See also Thomas Worcester, SJ, *Seventeenth-Century Cultural Discourse: France and the Preaching of Bishop Camus* (Berlin/New York: Mouton de Gruyter, 1997).

5. Camus, *The Spirit of Francis de Sales*, pp. 56–7.

6. It has been questioned whether Camus is a reliable witness to the real de Sales. Alexander T. Pocetto, OSFS, argues in his unpublished 2001 Salesian Scholars seminar paper, 'Jean-Pierre Camus (1584–1652) as Disseminator of the Salesian Spirit', that he is. The

original version of Camus' work appeared from 1639 to 1641. Pierre Collot made an abridged version of it in 1727.

7. The first printed text of the deposition was published in *Divers supplements aux oeuvres de Saint François de Sales* (Lyons; 1837) by Abbé de Baudry of Geneva. For the English translation of it and of the long letter to Goulu, see *St Francis de Sales: A Testimony by St Chantal*. See also Stopp, 'A Character Sketch of St Francis de Sales'.

8. *St Francis de Sales: A Testimony by St Chantal*, pp. 113–14.

9. Ibid., pp. 114–15. Francis' father died in 1610, his brothers Gallois and Bernard (Marie-Aymée's husband) in 1614 and 1617 respectively. His sister Jeanne succumbed in 1607 in Burgundy while under Jane's care.

10. Jane's initial letter served as the introduction to Veuillot's 1865 collection of the *Letters of Francis de Sales* and Sainte Beuve, the historian of Port Royal, claimed in 1861 that Jane's portrait was masterful. However, her portrait did not reach as wide an audience as did Camus'.

11. See Elisabeth Stopp, *Hidden in God* for a thorough discussion of changing portraits of Jane over the centuries.

12. *A Hundred Letters from the Correspondence of Jeanne Chézard de Matel*, ed. Kathleen McDonagh, IWBS (Corpus Christi, Texas: Sisters of the Incarnate Word and Blessed Sacrament, 1994).

13. Mère de Chaugy's *Mémoire* is found in vol. 1 of *Sa vie et ses oeuvres*. On François-Madeleine see Ernestine Lecouturier, *Françoise Madeleine de Chaugy et la tradition Salésienne au XVIIᵉ siècle* (Paris: Bloud et Gay, 1933), and Marie-Patricia Burns, VHM, *Françoise Madeleine de Chaugy: dans l'ombre et la lumière de la canonisation de François de Sales* (Annecy: Académie Salésienne, 2002).

14. *Sa vie et ses oeuvres*, p. 135.

15. The alterations are found mostly in the third segment where the bishop added his own headings and a string of maxims quoted from Mother de Chantal. See Stopp, *Hidden in God*, p. 511ff.

16. Cf. André Ravier's introduction to the Pléiade edition, *Saint François de Sales: Oeuvres*, pp. 3–15. Ravier in 1969 noted that no one in the nineteenth or twentieth centuries seems to have kept track of subsequent editions. That appears still to be the case.

17. Elisabeth Stopp, *A Man to Heal Differences: Essays and Talks on St Francis de Sales* (Philadelphia: St Joseph's University Press, 1997), 85ff. See also William C. Marceau, 'Early English Translations of Salesian Writings', *Indian Journal of Spirituality*, 8:2 (June 1995), 155–64.

18. *Oeuvres*, Pléiade, p. 14.

19. Francis de Sales, *Introduction to the Devout Life*, trans. Missionaries of St Francis de Sales (Bangalore, India: SFS Publications, 1990), Preface, p. 1–2.

20. *Introduction*, II, Ch. 12, trans. John K. Ryan (New York: Doubleday Image, 1950), p. 82.
21. Ibid., II, 7, p. 86. The 'spiritual bouquet' is a Salesian variant of the Ignatian examen that was to be practised at the end of each day.
22. Ibid., III, pp. 1, 117–18.
23. Ibid., III, pp. 19, 171.
24. Ibid., III, pp. 38, 216.
25. The *Treatise* was first published in 1616. Francis actually began work on it before he wrote the more popular *Introduction*, which was first published in 1607. There are a number of manuscript variants that make a critical study challenging. See André Ravier's introduction in the Pléiade edition of the *Oeuvres*, 1417–1582. See also his introduction to *Entretiens spirituels*, pp. 975–96.
26. Jeanne de Chantal, *Correspondance*, Edition critique, établie et annoteé par Soeur Marie-Patricia Burns, VHM, VI Tomes (Alençon: Les Editions du Cerf Centre d'études Franco-Italien des Universités de Turin et de Savoie, 1986–1993).
27. The Bolandists' monumental work was not accepted without criticism and controversy.
28. R. Po-Chia Hsia, *The World of Catholic Renewal 1540–1770* (Cambridge: Cambridge University Press, 1998), pp. 122–137.
29. On the complex process that preceded the canonisation and the role of Mother de Chaugy see Burns, *Françoise Madeleine de Chaugy*.
30. On the changing views of Jane see Stopp, *Hidden in God*. Stopp points out that Henri Brémond's portrait of Jane is as imbalanced as Bougaud's in exaggerating her mysticism and characterising her as the bold leader in prayer in their friendship. Stopp applauds Hamon's 1850 biography and Vicomte Emmanuel de Jeu's 1927 *Madame de Chantal*. Stopp herself wrote what remains the very best biography to this day. Her *Madame de Chantal: Portrait of a Saint* (London: Faber and Faber, 1962) was reprinted by De Sales Resource Center in 2002.
31. See William Thompson's introduction to *Bérulle and the French School: Selected Writings*, trans. Lowell M. Glendon, SS (Mahwah, NJ: Paulist Press, 1989), pp. 39–40.
32. Ibid., p. 40.
33. Raymond Deville, *The French School of Spirituality: An Introduction and a Reader*, trans. Agnes Cunningham (Pittsburgh: Duquesne University Press, 1994), p. 10.
34. 1914 *Catholic Encyclopedia*, 'French Congregation of the Oratory'.
35. Cf. *Saint Jean Eudes*, introduction et choix de texts par Paul Milcent (Paris: Bloud et Gay, 1964), pp 33–6.
36. Eudes' devotion owes nothing to Visitandine Margaret Mary's visionary version of the Sacred Heart for Eudes' veneration precedes hers and is drawn from the common fund of popular Heart devotion current at the time.

37. The constitutions of Our Lady of Charity were also based on the Visitation constitutions. See Charles Lebrun, *La spiritualité de Saint Jean Eudes* (Paris: P. Lethielleux, 1933), p. 18.

38. The Visitation team, led by a Mother Patia, only gradually came to accept their role in the establishment of Our Lady of Charity of the Refuge. For a period they withdrew, then accepted their leadership role which they exercised for over twenty years. Eventually, the new institute supplied its own leadership. See Clément Guillon, CJM, *In All Things the Will of God: Saint John Eudes Through His Letters*, trans. Louis Levesque, CJM (Buffalo, NY: St John Eudes Center, 1994). The Refuge Sisters were more than circumstantially formed by the Visitation spirit. Eudes not only felt that the spirituality of the group should be Salesian, he also intended the group to reflect the novel structure of the Visitation, with each house autonomously administered and joined to all others only through bonds of love. Likewise, Eudes drew Salesian inspiration from the Visitation as he composed the constitutions for the Congregation of Jesus and Mary (see Lebrun, *La spiritualité de Saint Jean Eudes*, p. 11). The more familiar modern community, Our Lady of Charity of the Good Shepherd (the Good Shepherd Sisters), is a branch of the group founded by Eudes.

39. *Vincent de Paul and Louise de Marillac: Rules, Conferences and Writings*, ed. Frances Ryan, DC and John E. Rybolt, CM (Mahwah, NJ: Paulist Press, 1995), p. 21.

40. Ibid., p. 127.

41. Ibid., p. 158.

42. *Spiritual Writings of Louise de Marillac: Correspondence and Thoughts*, trans. Louise Sullivan, DC (Albany, NY: New City Press, 1991), p. 1–2.

43. Ibid., p. 69.

44. Ibid., p. 704.

45. On Bonal see Marcellin Rigal, *Raymond Bonal et son oeuvre: les premiers seminaires dans le Midi de la France* (Rodez: Societé des Lettres, Sciences et Arts de l'Aveyron, 1966).

46. Ibid., p. 34.

47. Francis' heart was removed from his body and, as was the custom, enshrined and venerated separately. See Pedro Fernando Rodriguez, OP, *The Heart of St Francis de Sales in the Visitation Convent of Treviso* (Treviso: GMV Libri, 2002).

48. Ibid., p. 65.

49. Ibid., p. 74.

50. Jacques Le Brun, 'La Visitation et la spiritualité du pur amour au temps de la querelle du quietisme', in *Visitation et Visitandines*, pp. 441–60.

51. See also William C. Marceau, CSB, 'Fénelon – Epigone of St Francis de Sales' in *Salesian Insights*, pp. 103–113.

52. James Kelly, 'Madame Guyon (1648–1717)' in *Spirituality*, 5:22 (January-February, 1999), 30–33.
53. On Bossuet and Francis see Jean-Pierre Landry, 'Panégyriques de Saint François de Sales par Bossuet, Bourdaloue et Fléchier: le regard de la génération classique', and Thérèse Goyet, ' "Notre Mère La Providence" ou la methode salésienne lue par Bossuet', in *l'Unidivers salésien*, pp. 377–90 and pp. 363–73.

Chapter 5: Behold This Heart!:
Margaret Mary Alacoque and the Sacred Heart

1. *The Letters of St Margaret Mary Alacoque: Apostle of the Sacred Heart*, trans. from the 1920 French Gauthey edition by Fr Clarence A. Herbst, SJ (Rockford, Illinois: TAN Books, 1997), pp. 125–27.
2. On the image of the heart in the Visitation before Margaret Mary, see especially Hélène Bordes and Jean Marie Lemaire, 'L'oraison Visitandine et les sources de Marguerite-Marie', and Henri L'Honoré, 'Le culte du Coeur du Christ à la Visitation avant Marguerite-Marie' in *Sainte Marguerite-Marie et le message de Paray-le-Monial*, sous la responsabilité de R. Darricau-B. Peyrous (Paris: Desclée, 1993), pp. 75–118 and 119–32.
3. *Oeuvres*, XV, pp. 15, 63–4.
4. *Francis de Sales, Jane de Chantal: Letters of Spiritual Direction*, pp. 261–2.
5. On the iconography of the early Visitation see Hélène Bordes and Jean Marie Lemaire, 'Quelque aspects de la premier inconographie du Coeur de Jésus', in *Sainte Marguerite-Marie et le message de Paray-le-Monial*, pp. 349–76.
6. Visitandines have had varying interpretations of the initials MA on the cross they wear. *Mater Admirabilis, Mater Amabilis, Mons Amoris* have all been suggested. Hélène Bordes in her 'Quelques aspects de la premiere iconographie du Coeur de Jesus', p. 355, has shown that the Visitandine cross is similar to that of Francis' own cross, which bore the letters MAR for Mary. In the Visitandine version the A is covered over by the heart. Bordes suggests that this was meant to evoke the exchange of hearts between Mary and her Son.
7. *Oeuvres*, XV, pp. 15, 63–4.
8. The critical sources for Margaret Mary are *Vie et oeuvres de Marguerite-Marie*, présentations de Professeur R. Darricau (Paris: Fribourg: Editions St Paul, 1991), 2 vols. For seminal recent studies of the saint see the R. Darricau et B. Peyrous volume *Saint Marguerite-Marie et le message de Paray-le-Monial*. See too Jean Ladame, *La Sainte de Paray: Marguerite-Marie* (Montsurs: Editions Résiac, 1986).
9. Classic histories and more recent studies of the devotion are Rev. J.

V. Bainvel, SJ, *Devotion to the Sacred Heart: The Doctrine and It's History* (London: Burns, Oates and Washburn, 1924), *Faith in Christ and the Worship of Christ*, ed. Leo Scheffczyk, trans. Graham Harrison (San Francisco: Ignatius Press, 1986), and *Heart of the Saviour: A Symposium on Sacred Heart Devotion*, ed. Joseph Stierli, trans. Paul Andrews (New York: Herder and Herder, 1958). On other spiritual writers and the image see *Spiritualities of the Heart*, ed. Annice Callahan. It is also significant to note that the era in which the Salesian founders lived has been described as an era in which, across the denominational and interfaith divide, 'religions of the heart' flourished. See Ted A. Campbell, *The Religion of the Heart: A Study of European Religious Life in the Seventeenth and Eighteenth Centuries* (Columbia, SC: University of South Carolina Press, 1991). For a contemporary meditation focused on the history of the heart symbol see Wendy M. Wright, *Sacred Heart: Gateway to God* (Maryknoll, NY: Orbis/London: Darton, Longman and Todd, 2001).

10. For an English translation see *The Sacred Heart of Jesus by Saint John Eudes*, trans. Dom. Richard Flower, OSB (New York: Kenedy and Sons, 1946).

11. *Vie et oeuvres de Marguerite-Marie*, 1:82. On the different versions of this report see Edouard Glotin, 'Un Jour de Saint Jean l'Evangeliste', in *Sainte Marguerite-Marie et le message de Paray-le-Monial*, pp. 211–65.

12. See Marilyn Masse, 'La Visitation et la dévotion an Sacré-Coeur', in *Visitation et Visitandines*, pp. 461–82 and E. Glotin, 'Sainte Marguertie-Marie et les Jésuites' in *Sainte Marguerite-Marie et le message de Paray-le-Monial*, pp. 323–48.

13. Masse, 'La devotion au Sacré-Coeur,' p. 469.

14. *The Letters of St Margaret Mary Alacoque: Apostle of the Sacred Heart*, trans. Clarence A. Herbst, SJ reprint of the 1954 English edition (Rockford, IL: Tan Books, 1997), pp. 222–3.

15. Margaret Mary's autobiography is found in a critical edition in volume I of the 1991 *Vie et oeuvres de Marguerite-Marie*. See also *Sainte Marguerite-Marie: Sa Vie par elle-même* (Paris: Editions Saint Paul, 1979). English translations include *Autobiography of St Margaret Mary Alacoque*, reprint of the 1930, trans. Visitandine Sisters of Kent/Partridge Green (Rockford, IL: Tan Books, 1986). The influential nineteenth-century French biography by Émile Bougaud has also been reprinted as *The Life of Saint Margaret Mary Alacoque*, trans. Visitandine of Baltimore (Rockford, IL: TAN Books, 1990).

16. Cf. E. Glotin, 'Sainte Marguerite-Marie et les Jésuites' especially on the contribution of Croiset. For an English translation of his work: John Croiset, *The Devotion to the Sacred Heart of Our Lord Jesus Christ*, trans. from the French pub. at Lyons in 1694 by Patrick O'Connell (Westminster, MD: Newman Press, 1948).

17. The fascinating tale of the Sacred Heart and the French monarchy is told in detail in Raymond Jonas, *France and the Cult of the Sacred Heart: An Epic Tale for Modern Times* (Berkeley and Los Angeles: University of California Press, 2000).

18. *I Leave You My Heart: A Visitandine Chronicle of the French Revolution: Mother Marie Jeronyme Verot's Letter of 15 May 1794*, trans. Péronne-Marie Thibert, VHM (Philadelphia: Saint Joseph's University Press, 1999).

19. Etienne Catta, *La Vie d'un monastère sous l'ancien régime: La Visitation Sainte-Marie de Nantes* (1630–1792) (Paris: J. Vrin, 1954), pp. 465–66. Quoted in *I Leave You My Heart*, pp. 15–16.

Chapter 6: The Nineteenth-Century Salesian Pentecost

1. *Treatise on the Love of God*, book 10, chapter 11.

2. Francis' feast is celebrated on 24 January. Jane's has been moved several times. Presently it is celebrated in the United States, Central and South America on 18 August (so it will not conflict with Our Lady of Guadalupe, Patroness of the Americas). In the rest of the world it is observed on 12 December.

3. Ralph Gibson, *A Social History of French Catholicism 1789–1914* (New York: Routledge, 1989). Gibson characterises the Tridentine Catholicism that dominated the eighteenth century as a demanding, clerically dominated intellectual's religion, hostile to popular culture, which taught a rigid morality, a *contemptus mundi*, and which imposed itself by means of the threat of damnation. When Francis de Sales and Jane de Chantal were beginning their community, the dictates of Trent had yet to be fully implemented in France. Further, the synthesis that can be characterised as 'Tridentine Catholicism' did not emerge in the French church until later in the seventeenth century.

4. Thomas A. Kselman, *Miracles and Prophecies in Nineteenth Century France* (Brunswick, New Jersey: Rutgers University Press, 1983), stresses that the appearance of phenomena like miracles, stigmata and Marian apparitions was in response to a modern society that threatened to destroy the sacred canopy of traditional religious symbols. The emphasis on redemptive suffering and the importance of 'victim souls' was related to the perceived guilt of the modern era, while the ideals of poverty, simplicity and humility held up in idealised portraits of saints functioned as a critique of modernity's unbridled pursuit of wealth, rationalism and social protest. The increased affective quality of devotion might be seen as a parallel to the Romantic movement as well as a part of a gradual rejection of the stern, punitive religious emphasis that had dominated the Tridentine Church.

5. See *Alphonsus Liguori: Selected Writings,* edited by Frederick M. Jones, CSSR (New York/Mahwah: Paulist Press, 1999).
6. For a discussion of the differences between Liguori and de Sales and the way in which seventeenth-century piety contrasts with later expressions of devotion see Ann Taves, *The Household of Faith: Roman Catholic Devotions in Mid-Nineteenth Century America* (Notre Dame: University of Notre Dame Press, 1987), p. 71ff. As an example, while Francis stressed that the emotions generated by meditation should be directed to ethical action, the Redemptorist used meditations to form bonds of affection between human and supernatural beings.
7. Henri l'Honoré, OSFS, 'Ramifications de la famille Salésienne', *L'Unidivers Salésien,* pp. 459–71.
8. Among the groups not treated here but which are sheltered under the umbrella of the Salesian family, especially those associated with Don Bosco's communities are: Figlie di S. Fracesco di Sales or Daughters of Francis de Sales (Ravenna Italy, 1872); Salesias or Sisters of Saint Francis de Sales (Venice, 1751); World Federations of Past Pupils of Don Bosco and of Mary Help of Christians; Secular Institute of the Volunteers of Don Bosco; Daughters of the Sacred Hearts of Jesus and Mary (Colombia, founded 1910/official recognition 1983); Salesian Oblates of the Sacred Heart (Italy, 1933/1983); Sisters Apostles of the Holy Family (Italy, 1889/1984); Caritas Sisters of Miyazaki (Japan, 1937/1986); Missionary Sisters of Mary Help of Christians (India, 1942/1986); Handmaids of the Immaculate Heart of Mary (Thailand, 1937/1987); Daughters of the Divine Savior (El Salvador, 1956/1987); Daughters of Jesus Adolescent (Brazil, 1938/1987); Association of Salesian Ladies (Venezuela, 1968/1988); Catechist Sisters of Mary Immaculate and Help of Christians (India, 1948/1992). Other groups begun on the initiative of Salesians: Sisters of the Announcers of the Lord (Hong Kong, 1931); Pious Union of Mary Mazzarello (Argentina, 1939); Josephine Daughters (Brazil, 1949); Daughters of the Queenship of Mary (Thailand, 1954); Daughters of Mary Co-Redemptrix (Italy, 1956); Parish Missionaries of Mary Help of Christians (Dominican Republic, 1961); Missionaries of the Good Jesus (Brazil, 1964); Mediator Daughters of Peace (Brazil, 1968); Daughters of the Resurrection (Guatemala, 1977); Visitation Sisters of Don Bosco (India, 1983). Spin-offs of the Visitation community are also manifold and include Mother Louise-Margaret Claret de la Touche's 'Bethany of the Sacred Heart' (1918); Sisters of the Visitation of the Congregation of the Immaculate Heart of Mary (Iowa, 1952); Whitewater Community (Colorado, 1978).
9. Francis Moget, MSFS, *The Missionaries of St Francis de Sales of Annecy* (Bangalore, India: SFS Publications, 1985), p. 89.
10. The most authoritative book on the MSFS is Moget. I follow him in this discussion.

11. Moget, *The Missionaries of St Francis*, p. 25.
12. Ibid., p. 29.
13. The two congregations functioned under one superior general until 1887 when they were independently established.
14. Unlike the Holy Cross community, the early Visitation drew most of its recruits from the upper classes. Roger Devos in his *Les Visitandines d'Annecy* suggests that the Second monastery in Annecy was established to take care of lower class entrants while the First housed upper-class women.
15. The Missionaries today run a publishing house that continues to reprint and produce original works on St Francis de Sales and other Salesian themes.
16. Moget, *The Missionaries of St Francis*, pp. 88–90.
17. I am aware that members of the Don Bosco family especially might find it odd to see themselves depicted as one of many spiritual currents stemming from the seventeenth-century Salesian founders. While Bosco himself was a Piedmontese and steeped in de Sales' thought, the communities he founded look more to him as the source of their spirit than to his predecessors. Nevertheless, many of the master metaphors that guide their spiritual orientation, though certainly not all of them, can be found in Francis and Jane. In this section I am indebted to the scholarship and guidance of Joseph Boenzi, SDB, and follow his lead in this section on Don Bosco. However, I take responsibility for any errors or disputable interpretations. See also Arnaldo Pedrini, SDB, *St Francis de Sales: Don Bosco's Patron: St Francis de Sales in the Times, Life and Thought of St John Bosco* (New Rochelle, NY: Don Bosco Publications, 1988).
18. Giovanni Battista Lemoyne, *The Biographical Memoirs of Saint John Bosco*, trans. Diego Borgatello (New Rochelle: Salesiana Pub., 1966), 3:68. The anastatic reprint of Don Bosco's published works (he published from 1884 untl the late 1880s) is in 38 volumes. Giovanni Bosco, *Opere edite*, Ristampa anastatica, vols. 1–37, Prima Serie: Libri e Opuscoli, Centro Studi Don Bosco, Universita Pontificia Salesiana (Roma: LAS, 1976–77) and *Opere edite*, Ristampa anastatica, vol. 38, Seconda Serie: Contributi su giornali e periodici, Studi Don Bosco, Universita Pontificia Salesiana (Roma: LAS, 1987). Critical editions of Bosco's unpublished works continue. See also Giovanni Battista Lemoyne, Angelo Amadei and Eugenio Ceria, *Memorie Biografiche di Don Giovanni Bosco*, 19 vol. (S. Benigno Canavese/Torino: Tipografia Salesiana, 1897–1917). Included in the critical edition of Don Bosco's works are *Constituzioni della Societa di S. Francesco di Sales* [1858]-1875, intro. and notes Francesco Motto, Instituto Storico Salesiano, Fonti, Series I: Giovanni Bosco, *Scritti Editi e Inediti*, no. 1 (Roma: LAS 1982); *Epistolario*, vol. 1 (1835–1863), intro. and notes Francesco Motto, Instituto Storico Salesiano, Fonti, 1–6 (Roma: LAS, 1991); *Epistolario*, vol. 2

(1864–1868), intro. and notes Francesco Motto, Instituto Storico Salesiano, Fonti, 1–8 (Roma: LAS, 1996); *Memorie della Oratorio di S. Francesco di Sales: Dal 1815–1855*, critical edition Antonio Da Silva Ferreira (Roma: LAS, 1991); *Scritti pedagogici e spirtuali*, ed. Piero Braido, Instituto Storico Salesiano, Fonti, 1–3 (Roma: LAS, 1987). The American translation done at Salesiana in New Rochelle (1964 –) consists at present of 17 volumes.

19. In fact, the members of the royal family of Savoy – Amedeus VIII (1383–1451) and Amadeus IX (1435–1472) – a pious and just ruler – were the most commonly admired local heroes at the time.

20. Giuseppe Cafasso, *Instruzioni per Esercizi Spirituali al Clero*, edited by Giuseppe Allamano (Turino: Canonica, 1893), p. 309. (Trans. Joseph Boenzi, SDB).

21. Lemoyne, *Memorie Biografiche*, 1:518.

22. The Penitent Sisters of Saint Mary Magdalene included among them women who had been rescued from the streets. The rule of life they adopted was modelled on the Visitation constitutions. They lived a life of simplicity as described in the *Introduction to the Devout Life*.

23. S. Giovanni Bosco, *Memoirs of the Oratory of Saint Francis de Sales from 1815 to 1855: The Autobiography of Saint John Bosco*, trans. David Lyons (New Rochelle, NY: Don Bosco Publications, 1989), pp. 216–19. This edition has commentaries and an extended critical bibliography on John Bosco, his method and society. Other English language sources on Don Bosco are Augustine Auffray, SDB, *Saint John Bosco*, trans. from French of 1930 (Blaisdon, England: Salesian Publications, 1964); *The Spiritual Writings of Saint John Bosco*, translation by Joseph Caselli (New Rochelle: Don Bosco Publications, 1984); Eugenio Ceria, *Don Bosco With God*, trans. Hugh McGlenchey, SDB (Madras: Salesian Publications, n.d.); Francis Desramaut, *Don Bosco and the Spiritual Life*, trans. Roger M. Luna (Don Bosco, 1979).

24. Pedrini, p. 21. From the *Biographic Memoires of St John Bosco*.

25. *Memoirs of the Oratory*, p. 217.

26. Arthur Lenti, 'Don Bosco's Love Affair with "Poor and Abandoned" Young People and the Beginnings of the Oratory', in *The Journal of Salesian Studies*, VI: 1 (Spring 1995), 9. *The Journal of Salesian Studies* contains a wealth of current and seminal studies on the Salesians of Don Bosco as well as book reviews in the field.

27. Ibid., p. 19. The 'preventive system' was not really a system nor 'preventive'. It was at root formation in the Christian life according to the vision of the Salesian world of hearts. On this, see Francis Desramaut, *Les cents mots-clefs de la spiritualité Salésienne* (Paris: Editions Don Bosco, 2000), p. 501ff.

28. The lay Co-operators' purpose was simple: Christian spiritual formation achieved in the process of active service.

29. S. Giovanni Bosco, 'The "Rules" Given by Don Bosco to the Cooper-

ators', in *Regulations of Apostolic Life*, Association of Salesian Cooperators, trans. George Williams (Roma: Tipografia Don Bosco, 1995), 88, art. 1.

30. See Cf. Tullo Goffi, *La spiritualità dell'Ottocento* (Bologna: Edizione Behoniane, 1989), p. 312.

31. The nun at home was an ideal promoted by Alphonsus Liguori.

32. For an English language popular life see Domenico Agasso, *Saint Mary Mazzarello: The Spirit of Joy*, trans. Sr Louise Passero, FMA, (Boston: Pauline Books & Media, 1993). The *Journal of Salesian Studies* is a good resource for scholarly articles on the collaboration between Don Bosco and women.

33. See Edna Mary MacDonald, FMA, 'Towards a Theology of the Body: An Analysis of the Letters of Maria Dominica Mazzarello', *Journal of Salesian Studies*, VIII: 2 (Fall 1997), 310–31. Mother Mazzarello's autobiographical works consist of 68 known letters written between 1874–1881. Three Italian editions (1975, 1980, 1994) have been published. The only English translation is a 1978 one: *Letters of St Maria Domenica Mazzarello Cofoundress of the Institute of the Daughters of Mary Help of Christians*, trans. from the original (Shillong: Auxilium, 1978).

34. Quoted in McDonald, 'Toward a Theology of the Body,' p. 328.

35. Jack Ayers, 'The "Salesianity" that Wins Hearts', *Journal of Salesian Studies*, III:2 (Fall 1992), 1–22.

36. From Ségur's *Le renoncement* quoted in Marthe de Hedouville, *Monseigneur de Ségur: Sa vie-son action 1820–1881* (Paris: Nouvelles Éditions Latines, 1957), p. 287.

37. Ibid., p. 87.

38. Ibid., p. 305.

39. From Ségur's letters, quoted in Ibid., p. 333. Hedouville goes into great detail describing Francis de Sales' contributions to Ségur's thought and the way in which their pastoral practices were aligned and contrasted somewhat.

40. As well as supporting the Association of St Francis de Sales and like initiatives, Mermillod was instrumental in bringing to light de Sales' virtually forgotten manuscript, alternately called *Meditations on the Church* or *The Controversies*. This was a compilation of writings that Francis had done while on mission in the Chablais. See Elisabeth Stopp's essay, 'Meditations on the Church', in *A Man to Heal Differences*, pp. 51–74 and Blandine Delahaye, 'La Diffusion des Controverses pendant la mission du Chablais', in *L'Unidivers Salesien*, pp. 68–70.

41. Article 'Louis Gaston de Ségur', Catholic Encyclopedia, 1913 edition.

42. Hedouville, *Monsigneur de Ségur*, p. 464.

43. The custom of preserving and displaying the heart of a notable person was very common at the time. On this see Jean Nagle, *La*

civilization du Coeur: histoire du sentiment politique en France du XIIᵉ and XIXᵉ siècle (Librairie Arthème Favard, 1998).

44. Thérèse's maternal aunt and one sister, Léonie, were Visitandine nuns at, respectively, LeMans and Caens. Her remaining sisters Pauline and Marie, both of whom lived with her in the Lisieux Carmelite cloister, had boarded at the Visitation School where their aunt lived. Pauline, who became young Thérèse's second mother after their own mother's death, guided her little sister through letters saturated with unmistakably Salesian imagery – spiritual bouquets, the little virtues, and the heart of Jesus. Thérèse's own correspondence reveals her formation in the wisdom of Francis de Sales and her unique teaching on 'spiritual childhood' echoes with Salesian resonance. Her later spiritual guides within the Carmel, especially Mother Marie de Gonzaga, was also a product of Visitation schooling at Caen. And as a spiritual guide herself, especially in her letters to her troubled sister Léonie, Thérèse reveals her deep affinity with the tradition of the heart as it emerged after Margaret Mary Alacoque. On this, see Wendy M. Wright, 'A Salesian Pentecost: Léonie Aviat and Salesian Tradition', *Studies in Spirituality* 12 (2002), pp. 156–77.

45. *Saint Thérèse of Lisieux by Those Who Knew Her: Testimonies from the Process of Beatification*, trans. Christopher O'Mahoney, OCD, (Huntington, IN: Our Sunday Visitor, 1975), p. 180.

46. On Chaumont, see Debout, *Le chanoine Henri Chaumont et la sanctification du prêtre* (Paris, 1930), and Mgr Laveille, *L'abbé Henri Chaumont: fondateur de trois societés Salesiennes (1838–1896)* (Paris: Téqui, 1919).

47. Laveille, *L'abbé Henri Chaumont*, p. 165.

48. Ibid., p. 240. See also Laveille's *Vie de Madame Carré de Malberg*.

49. Chaumont had a special devotion to the Holy Spirit and this became part of the Daughters' spiritual inheritance. See Lavielle, *L'abbé Henri Chaumont*, p. 345ff.

50. From a brochure for the Daughters of St Francis de Sales, n.p., n.d.

51. Hedouville, *Monseigneur de Ségur*, p. 18.

52. From a June 1899 colloquy by Fr Brisson. Quoted in *The Constitutions and the Spiritual Directory of the Oblates of St Francis de Sales* (Oblates of Francis de Sales, 1964), p. 157.

53. Gibson, *A Social History of French Catholicism*, pp. 174–6.

54. On Marie-Thérèse de Sales Chappuis see the life by Louis Brisson, *Vie de la Vénérée Mère Marie de Sales Chappuis de l'ordre de la Visitation de Sainte-Marie* (Paris: Chez l'Aumonie de la Visitation, 1891) and the much shorter *The Venerable Mary de Sales Chappuis of the Order of the Visitation Holy Mary 1793–1875* by the Sisters of the Visitation, Brooklyn (Brooklyn, NY: Sisters of the Visitation, 1924), as well as Mère Marie de Bellaing, *Abrégé de la vie et des vertus de notre très honoré et véneré Mère-Marie de Sales Chappuis*

(Troyes, n.d., n.l.), English translation, *Abridgement of the Life of the Venerable Mother Mary de Sales Chappuis* (Brooklyn, NY: n.p., n.d.). I am indebted to Alexander Pocetto, OSFS, for his research on the Good Mother gathered together in his unpublished 2002 seminar paper, 'Mary de Sales Chappuis (1793–1875), Apostle of the Salesian Spirit'.

55. *The Little Notebook of Fribourg (Le Petit Cahier de Fribourg)*, analysis, translation and commentary by Edward Carney, OSFS (Private printing, n.p., n.d.), p. 38. See too Marie de Sales Chappuis, *Le petit cahier de Fribourg*, ed. Roger Balducelli, OSFS (Troyes: private printing, 2000).

56. *Oeuvres*, pp. 6, 90–91. (Trans. Alexander Pocetto, OSFS).

57. Louis Brisson, *Retraites de l' Année 1890*, p. 2.

58. *Abridgement of the Life*, p. 117–18.

59. *The Venerable Mother Mary de Sales Chappuis*, p. 99. The quotes from the *Pensées* are not footnoted. I have modernised the English translation of these *Pensées*.

60. Ibid., pp. 101–2.

61. Ibid., p. 98.

62. The cause of the Good Mother was introduced in the late nineteenth century. Due to a complex set of unfortunate circumstances, her writings fell under suspicion. For a view that reclaims her good name and the soundness of her teaching see Roger Balducelli, OSFS, *The Cause for the Beatification of the Venerable Mother de Sales Chappuis*, trans. Alexander Pocetto, OSFS (*International Commission on Salesian Spirituality*, Oblates of St Francis de Sales, 2000).

63. Biographies of Brisson include Katherine Burton, *So Much So Soon: Father Brisson, Founder of the Oblates of St Francis de Sales* (New York: Benzinger Bros., 1953), Prosper Dufour, OSFS, *Le Très Révérend Père Louis Brisson, fondateur des Oblates et Oblats de Saint François de Sales (1817–1908)* (Paris: Desclée de Brouwer, 1936).

64. *Cor ad Cor: Meditations for Every Day of the Year from the Teachings of Father Louis Brisson*, trans. Joseph E. Woods, OSFS (Philadelphia: William T. Cooke Publishing, 1955), p. 25.

65. Ibid., p. 28.

66. Ibid., p. 30.

67. Ibid., pp. 34–5.

68. The foundation of the Oblates is surrounded by prophecy and miracle that seems not simply to be the product of pious hindsight. Mother de Sales Chappuis did have some sort of prophetic and clairvoyant capacities. See her biography and Brisson's on this.

69. On Mother Aviat, see Marie-Aimée D'Esmauges, *M'oublier entièrement: Léonie Aviat, Mère Françoise de Sales, 1844–1914* (Sainte-Savine: l'Imprimerie COVAM, 1991)/ *To Forget Myself Entirely: Léonie Aviat, Mère Françoise de Sales, 1844–1914*, trans. Oblate Sisters of Francis de Sales of Childs, Maryland (Wilmington, DE:

Litho Print, 1991). The above are both based on the life [Mère Aimée de Sales de Cissey], *Vie de la très Révérende Mère Françoise de Sales Aviat, Fondatrice de la congregation des Oblates de Saint Françoise de Sales* (Rome: Imprimerie Polyglotte Vaticane, 1928).

70. D'Esmauges, *To Forget Myself Entirely*, pp. 22–3.

71. Ibid., p. 56.

72. Ibid., p. 38.

73. Ibid., p. 88.

74. D'Esmauges, *M'oublier entièrement*, p. 121.

75. Ibid., p. 88.

76. 'Petits Cahiers' de Mère Françoise de Sales Aviat, Edition dactylographiée, quoted in D'Esmauges, *M'oublier entièrement*, p. 126.

77. On the Oblates, see especially Prosper Dufour, OSFS, *Les Oblats de Saint François de Sales* (Paris: Letouzey et Ane, 1933)/ *The Oblates of St Francis de Sales*, trans. Joseph Bowler, OSFS (Wilmington, DC: De Sales Publishing, 1994). Also see Louis Brisson, OSFS, *Chapitres, retraites et allocations*, ed. Jacob Langelaan, OSFS, 7 Vols. (Tilburg: Maison 'Ave Maria', 1966–68/ *Chapters by the venerable Father Louis Brisson, OSFS*, trans. Joseph D. Bowler, 7 Vols. (Center Valley, PA: Oblates of St Francis de Sales and Allentown College of St Francis de Sales, 1981–); Louis Brisson, OSFS, *Documents pour servir à l'histoire des Oblats de Saint François de Sales*, ed. Roger Balducelli, OSFS (Rome: Curia Generalizia, 1987)/ *Documents to be Used for the History of the Oblates of St Francis de Sales*, trans. Alexander Pocetto, OSFS (Rome: Generalate, 1987); *The Foundational Years: Letters and Documents 1867–1875*, ed. Roger Balducelli, OSFS (Rome: Curia Generalizia, 1994); *The Origins of the Congregations: Letters and Documents 1867-1875 (Texts and Studies Concerning the Origins of the Oblates of St Francis de Sales*, ed. Roger Balducelli, OSFS (Rome: Curia Generalizia, 1992). The Oblates sponsor the International Commission on Salesian Studies to disseminate information on the Salesian tradition. The ICSS publishes a newsletter which can be accessed on line at www.desales.edu/salesian/

78. The story of Brisson's long resistance to the Good Mother's prophetic gifts is a fascinating one. Eventually he was convinced that she could claim some special foreknowledge in regards to the priestly institute. This involved his disconcerting visionary apprehension of Jesus Himself and several seemingly miraculous proofs of his mission.

79. Formation in the present-day Oblates is still rooted in the *Spiritual Directory*. Oblates also look for guidance first to scripture, then to theology and the other works of Francis de Sales. As Saint Francis himself taught, once the formative work of the *Directory* is done and its intent internalised, its multitude of observances may be simplified.

80. Père Brisson, *St François de Sales: Commentaire du Directoire spiri-*

tuel à l'usage des Oblats de St François de Sales (Eichstätt: Imprimerie St François de Sales, 1935), pp. 3–4. On this see the study by Edward J. Carney, OSFS, *Fr. Brisson's Commentary on the Constitutions and the Spiritual Directory of the Oblates of St Francis de Sales* (Hyattsville, MD: Institute of Salesian Studies, 1966).

81. *Cor ad Cor*, p. 143.

82. Saint Louis Visitation Archives, 'Death Letter of Sr Evangelista Prince', 28 October 1922. No baptismal name indicated. I an indebted to Paula McCarthy, VHM, and Mary Grace McCormack, VHM, for their knowledge about the Visitation in America.

83. On English language works on the Salesian tradition, see the web-based bibliography by Fr Joseph Boenzi, SDB, 'Saint Francis de Sales: Toward a Complete Bibliography of English-language Works'. http://www4.desales.edu/~salesian/fdsbibli.html. See also William Charles Marceau, 'Early English Translations of Salesian Writings', *Indian Journal of Spirituality*, 8.2 (June 1995): 155–64; 8.3 (September 1995): 316–20.

84. An extended treatment of the Catholic Reformation-English metaphysical poetic traditions is found in Louis L. Martz, *The Poetry of Meditation: A Study in English Religious Literature of the Seventeenth Century* (New Haven/London: Yale University Press, 1954). Early Salesian influence across the channel is likewise treated by Elisabeth Stopp, in her 'Healing Differences: St Francis de Sales in Seventeenth Century England', in *A Man To Heal Differences*, pp. 85–118.

85. On the Visitation in England, see the monograph by Elisabeth Stopp, *Saint Francis de Sales and the Order of the Visitation* (Waldron, Sussex: Monastery of the Visitation, 1962). I am indebted to Sr Péronne Marie Thibert with her familiarity with the *Année Sainte* for the information about the hearts of the English royal family at Chaillot. Marie Beatrix even wanted her body to be buried at Chaillot until her son, James III would be re-established on the throne of England.

86. See for example, *The Life of Jeanne Charlotte de Bréchard of the Order of the Visitation: Friend and Spiritual Daughter of St Francis de Sales and St Jane-Frances de Chantal, 1580–1637* by Sisters of the Visitation, Harrow-on-the-Hill (New York/London: Longmans, Green and Co., 1924). See also the web-based bibliography by Fr Joseph Boenzi, SDB, 'Saint Francis de Sales: Toward a Complete Bibliography of English-language Works'. http://www4.desales.edu/~salesian/fdsbibli.html. for a list of English language works on Salesian topics, including those produced at Harrow-on-the-Hill.

87. On Mackey, see Joseph F. Power, OSFS, 'Henry Benedict Mackey, OSB: Nineteenth Century Interpreter of St Francis de Sales,' *Downside*

Review, vol. 120, no. 420 (July 2002), 215–28. This article contains a chronological bibliography of Mackey's work on de Sales.

88. For example, Dom John Chapman.

89. Power, 'Henry Benedict Mackey', p. 225.

90. The *Library of St Francis de Sales*, under the direction of John Cuthbert Hedley, OSB, contains the following volumes: I *Letters to Persons in the World* (London: Burns and Oates, 1883); II *Treatise on the Love of God* (London: Burns and Oates, 1884); III *The Catholic Controversy* (London: Burns and Oates, 1886); IV *Letters to Persons in Religion* (London: Burns and Oates, 1888); V *The Spiritual Conferences*, translated by Sisters of the Visitation Harrow-on-the-Hill (London: Burns and Oates/New York: Benziger Brothers, 1906); VI *The Mystical Explanation of the Canticle of Canticles by St Francis de Sales* and *The Deposition of St Jane Frances de Chantal in the Cause of the Canonization of St Francis de Sales* (London: Burns and Oates/New York: Benziger Brothers, 1980); VII *The Spirit of St Francis de Sales*, by his friend Jean Pierre Camus, trans. J. S. (London: Burns and Oates, 1910).

91. Power cites both John Ryan and Joseph Kerns as later translators who found Mackey's translations lacking.

92. See, for example, Dom B. Mackey, *St Francis de Sales as a Preacher: A Study*, trans. Thomas F. Dailey, OSFS (Bangalore, India: Indian Institute of Spirituality, n.d.).

93. Quoted in Power, 'Henry Benedict Mackey', p. 219.

94. Ibid., p. 220.

95. Elizabeth Bayley Seton, *Collected Writings*, ed. Regina Bechtle, SC, and Judith Metz, SC (New York: New City Press, 2000), Vol. 1 *Correspondence and Journals*, pp. 317–18.

96. Joseph I. Dirvin, *Mrs Seton: Foundress of the American Sisters of Charity* (New York: Ferrar, Strauss and Giroux, 1975), p. 139.

97. Ibid., p. 444.

98. Archives of St Joseph's provincial house, Emmitsburg, 1–3, 3–12:65a.

99. Taves, *The Household of Faith*, pp. 72–3.

100. Ibid., p. 9.

101. Joseph P. Chinnici, OFM, *Living Stones: The History and Structure of Catholic Spiritual Life in the United States* (New York: Macmillan Publishing, 1989), p. 30.

102. Ibid., p. 31.

103. Several of the Carmelites who came on this mission were American-born, had been sent abroad to be educated, and had entered religious life in Europe.

104. From Baltimore the Poor Clares moved to New Orleans then to Georgetown. Eventually they returned to France.

105. Eleanor C. Sullivan, *Georgetown Visitation: Since 1799* (Baltimore: French Bray Printing, 1975), p. 50. Sullivan's account is the most

accurate of the few printed accounts of the founding of the Visitation in the US Some of the US Visitation communities' histories have yet to be written and published. Others have been written. On Kaskaskia (St Louis) see *The Academy of the Visitation, St Louis, 1933: Centennial Souvenir* (St Louis: Sisters of the Visitation, 1933), and William B. Faherty, SJ, *Deep Roots and Golden Wings: One Hundred and Fifty Years with the Visitation Sisters in the Archdiocese of St Louis* (Saint Louis: River City Pub., 1983). On Frederick see *Centenary: Convent of the Visitation, Frederick, Maryland, 1846–1946* (Private printing, 1946). On Catonsville see Richard C. and Susan M. Randt, *The Academy of Every Virtue: a History of Mount de Sales Academy, Catonsville, Maryland* (Mount de Sales High School, 2001). On Keokuk (Wilmington/Tyringham) see *The Silver is Mine: a Brief History of St Joseph's Monastery of the Visitation in Wilmington, Delaware, Commemorating the First Centenary of Foundation from the Monastery of Montluel, France, 1853–1953* (Wilmington: Monastery of the Visitation, 1953). On Maysville, KY (Rock Island) see Katherine Burton, *Bells on Two Rivers: the History of the Visitation Sisters of Rock Island* (Milwaukee: Bruce Pub., 1965). On Richmond (Rockville) see *Sentinel on the Hill: Monte Marie and One Hundred Years* (Richmond: Monastery of the Visitation, 1966). On White Sulphur (Cardome) see Ann Bolton Bevins and Rev. James O'Rourke, *The Troublesome Parish: St Francis / St Pius Church of White Sulphur, Kentucky* (Georgetown, KY: St Francis and St John Parishes, 1985). On Mexico City (Philadelphia) see *River of Light: the Story of the Sisters of the Visitation of Philadelphia, PA* (Philadelphia: Monastery of the Visitation, 1963) and *Twice Called* (Philadelphia: Monastery of the Visitation, 1998). On Toledo see *This Foundation: a History of the Monastery of the Visitation, Toledo, Ohio, Golden Jubilee, 1915–1965* (Toledo, 1965). On Atlanta (Snellville) see Mary Helena O'Connell, VHM, *In the White Fields of Georgia: the Story of Rev. Mother Francis de Sales Cassidy and the Foundations of the Visitation in Georgia, 1954–79* (Snellville, 1979). The Georgetown archives especially contain a rich store of manuscripts, letters, and documents pertaining to American religious history.

106. Mada-anne Gell, VHM, '*Introduction to the Devout Life*: the First Rule of the Sisters of the Visitation in the United States', *Salesian Living Heritage*, IX: 2, 4–13.

107. Ibid., p. 56.

108. On the development of the order in the early years see Barbara Misner, SCSC, *A Comparative Social Study of the Members and Apostolates of the First Eight Permanent Communities of Women Religious Within the Original Boundaries of the United States 1790–1850*, Ph.D. dissertation at the Catholic University of America, Washington DC, 1980.

109. Alice Lalor, being Irish, had been educated at home as Ireland's schools were at the time closed to Catholics. Mrs McDermott is also said to have been educated at home by her father.
110. One of the interesting questions about the early school education concerned the education of poor black students. There is some indication that this took place in separate facilities. There is also indication that, like many of the day, the Visitation sisters for a time kept slaves. See Mada-anne Gell, VHM, 'Georgetown Visitation: The Myth of the Finishing School' in *Living Heritage*, vol. 1, no.1 (Sp. 1986), 29–42.
111. Ibid.
112. I am indebted to Sr Paula McCarthy VHM at the Visitation in Mendota Heights, Minnesota, for her chart that clarifies the complex history of foundations, relocations, mergers and closings of the various US Visitation houses. Few of the histories of the convents have been published or studied extensively. Monastery archives provide a wealth of documents that could enrich the history of American Catholicism. For example, the histories of many prominent families in many parts of the country are linked to the Visitation order. The Cox-Prince-Markoe family in France and America is a prime example. Documents are available in archives of the Mendota Heights Visitation.
113. Website for the Minneapolis Visitation. www.visitationmonastery.org/minneapolis/index.html
114. 'Life and Mission' statement from *A Possible Model for the Revision of the Constitutions, Juridical Directory and Federation Statues for the Visitation Sisters of the Visitation of Holy Mary*, unpublished document of the Second Federation, 1987.

Chapter 7: The Universal Call to Holiness: The Second Vatican Council and The Salesian Saints

1. Léon Joseph Cardinal Suenens, 'Saint François de Sales et Vatican II' in *Saint François de Sales, Témoignages et Mélanges, Mémoires et Documents* publiés par L'Académie Salésienne, Tome LXXX (Amabilly-Annemasse: Editions Franco-Swisses, 1968), pp. 23–4. Suenens, who was very influential in shaping the course of Vatican II, was himself a member of the Priests of Francis de Sales.
2. Pierre Serouet, article 'François de Sales', *Dictionnaire de Spiritualité ascétique et mystique*, Tome I, col. 1093. In this section on the Vatican Councils, I am relying on the unpublished research of the late Fr Joseph Power, OSFS.
3. Suenens, 'Saint François de Sales et Vatican II'.
4. Ibid.
5. Yves Congar, 'S. François de Sales aujourd'hui', in *Choisir*, (July-

Aug, 1962), 24–6. The short article appeared in English translation by Francis Sullivan, OSFS in *Salesian Studies* 3 (1966), 5–9.

6. Ibid., p. 9. Elisabeth Stopp has a more positive view of Francis as a 'proto-ecumenist'. See *A Man to Heal Differences*, pp. 193–202.

7. Put succinctly, in the incarnation she sees God's abasement while he sees the exaltation of humankind. Thus her emphasis is on the need to make reparation for sin while his is on achieving union. Margaret Mary reflects the Augustinian pessimism of her era.

8. For both a thorough explanation and a critique of the process see Kenneth Woodward, *Making Saints: How the Catholic Church Determines Who Becomes a Saint and Who Doesn't* (New York: Simon and Schuster, 1990).

9. On the Spanish martyrs see Martina Lopez, RA, *And They Gave Their Lives: the Seven Visitandine Martyrs of Madrid*, translated by Visitandines in the United States (Fremont, Ohio: Lesher Printers, 1997) and Robert Royal, *The Catholic Martyrs of the Twentieth Century* (New York: Crossroad, 2000), pp. 107–30.

10. Among these, but not limited to these, are these figures among Don Bosco's followers: Michael Rua, priest and successor to Bosco, Bishop Louis Versiglia, Callisto Caravario, priest and missionary, Laura Vicuña, Salesian student, Philip Rinaldi, priest, Maddaleno Morano, FMA, Maria Romero Meneses, FMA, Maria Romero, FMA, Luis Variara, priest, Artemides Zatti, Salesian brother, Dorotea Chopitea, Co-operator, August Czartoryski, priest, Andrew Beltrami, priest, Zeffirino Namiencura, youth, Teresa Valse, FMA, Vincent Cimatti, prefect apostolic, Simon Srugi, Coadjutor Salesian, Ruldolf Komorek, priest and missionary. Visitation sisters include Anne Madeleine Remuzat, Charlotte de Bréchard, and Marie de Sales Chappuis. Oblate Fathers and Brothers include Louis Brisson.

11. http://vatican.va/holy_father/john_paul . . . /hf_jp-ii_let_20021209_francesc-sales_fr.htm

ENGLISH LANGUAGE BIBLIOGRAPHY

Primary Sources:

Autobiography of Saint Margaret Mary Alacoque. Trans. Sisters of the Visitation. Rockford, IL: TAN Books, 1986.

Bosco, John. *Memoirs of the Oratory of Saint Francis de Sales from 1815 to 1855: the Autobiography of Saint John Bosco.* New Rochelle, NY: Don Bosco Pub., 1989.

Francis de Sales, Jane de Chantal: Letters of Spiritual Direction. Intro. Wendy M. Wright, Joseph F. Power, OSFS. Trans. Péronne-Marie Thibert, VHM. New York: Paulist Press, 1988.

Letters of Margaret Mary Alacoque: Apostle of the Sacred Heart. Trans. Clarence Herbst. Rockford, IL: TAN Books, 1997.

The Library of St Francis de Sales. Under the direction of John Cuthbert Hedley, OSB. Vol. I–IV trans. Henry Benedict Mackey. I: *Letters to Persons in the World* (London: Burns and Oates, 1883). II: *Treatise on the Love of God* (London: Burns and Oates, 1884). III: *The Catholic Controversy* (London: Burns and Oates, 1886). IV: *Letters to Persons in Religion* (London: Burns and Oates, 1888). V: *The Spiritual Conferences*, translated by Sisters of the Visitation, Harrow-on-the-Hill (London: Burns and Oates/New York: Benziger Brothers, 1906). VI: *The Mystical Explanation of the Canticle of Canticles by St Francis de Sales* and *The Deposition of St Jane Frances de Chantal in the Cause of the Canonization of St Francis de Sales* (London: Burns and Oates/New York: Benziger Brothers, 1980). VII: *The Spirit of St Francis de Sales*, by his friend Jean Pierre Camus, translated by J. S. (London: Burns and Oates, 1910).

On the Preacher and Preaching: A Letter by Francis de Sales. Trans. John K. Ryan. Chicago: Henry Regnery, 1964. Sales, Francis de. *Finding God Wherever You Are: Selected Spiritual Writings.* Ed. Joseph F. Power, OSFS. Hyde Park. NY: New City Press, 2000.

——. *Introduction to the Devout Life.* Trans. John K. Ryan. New York: Doubleday, 1982.

——. *Introduction to the Devout Life.* Trans. Armind Nazareth, OSFS, Antony Mookenthottam, OSFS, Antony Kolencherry, OSFS. Bangalore, India: SFS Publications., 1990.

——. *Spiritual Exercises*. Ed. Joseph F. Chorpenning, OSFS. Trans. William Dougherty. Toronto: Peregrina Pub., 1993.

——. *Treatise on the Love of God*. 2 Vol. Trans. John K. Ryan. Rockford, IL: TAN Books, 1974.

St Francis de Sales: The Mystical Exposition of the Canticle of Canticles. Trans. Thomas F. Dailey, OSFS. Center Valley, PA: Allentown College of St Francis de Sales, 1996.

St Francis de Sales: Selected Letters. Trans. Elisabeth Stopp. New York: Harper and Bros., 1960.

St Francis de Sales: A Testimony by Saint Chantal. Trans. Elisabeth Stopp. London: Faber and Faber, 1967.

Sermon Texts on Saint Joseph by Francis de Sales. Trans. and ed. Joseph F. Chorpenning, OSFS. Toronto: Peregrina Pub., 2000.

Sermons of St Francis de Sales. Ed. Lewis Fiorelli, OSFS. Trans. Sisters of the Visitation. Rockford, IL: TAN Books, 1985–87. 1: *On Prayer*. 2: *On Our Lady*. 3: *On Lent*. 4: *For Advent and Christmas*.

STUDIES

Abruzzese, John A. *The Theology of Hearts in the Writings of Saint Francis de Sales*. Rome: Institute of Spirituality, Pontifical University of St Thomas Aquinas, 1985.

Agnasso, Dominico. *Saint Mary Mazzarello: The Spirit of Joy*. Trans. Louise Passero, FMA. Boston: Pauline Books and Media, 1993.

Brisson, Louis. *Life of the Venerable Mother Marie de Sales Chappuis of the Order of the Visitation of Holy Mary*. Trans. Joseph D. Bowler, OSFS. Center Valley, PA: Oblates of Saint Francis de Sales, 1986.

Burton, Katherine. *So Much, So Soon: Father Brisson, Founder of the Oblates of St Francis de Sales*. New York: Benzinger Bros., 1953.

D'Esmauges, Marie-Aimée. *To Forget Myself Entirely: Léonie Aviat, Mother Frances de Sales, Foundress of the Oblate Sisters of St Francis de Sales*. Rome/Troyes: Oblate Sisters of Francis de Sales, 1991.

Desramaut, Francis. *Don Bosco and the Spiritual Life*. Trans. Roger P. Luna, SDB. New Rochelle, NY: Don Bosco Pub., 1979.

Koster, Dirk. *Francis de Sales*. Noorden, the Netherlands: Bert Post, 2000.

Lajeunie, E.-J., OP. *Saint Francis de Sales: the Man, the Thinker, His Influence*. 2 Vol. Trans. Rory O'Sullivan, OSFS. Bangalore, India: SFS Publications., 1987.

McGoldrick, Terence. *The Sweet and Gentle Struggle: Francis de Sales on the Necessity of Spiritual Friendship*. Lanham, MD: University Press of America, 1996.

Moget, Francis, MSFS. *The Missionaries of Saint Francis de Sales of Annecy*. Bangalore, India: SFS Publications, 1985.

Padrini, Arnoldo, SDB. *St Francis de Sales: Don Bosco's Patron*. New Rochelle, NY: Don Bosco Pub., 1988.

Ravier, André, SJ. *Francis de Sales: Sage and Saint.* Trans. Joseph D. Bowler. OSFS. San Francisco: Ignatius Press, 1988.

——. *St Jane de Chantal: Holy Lady, Noble Woman.* Trans. Mary Emily Hamilton. San Francisco: Ignatius Press, 1989.

Stopp, Elisabeth. *Hidden in God: Essays and Talks on St Jane Frances de Chantal.* Ed. Terence O'Reilly. Philadelphia: St Joseph's University Press, 1999.

——. *Madame de Chantal: Portrait of a Saint.* Westminster, MD: Newman Press, 1963. Reprinted: Stella Niagara, NY: De Sales Resource Center, 2002.

——. *A Man to Heal Differences: Essays and Talks on St Francis de Sales.* Philadelphia: St Joseph's University Press, 1997.

Streebling, Cecelian. *Devout Humanism as a Style: St François de Sales' Introduction à la vie dévote.* Washington: Catholic University of America Press, 1954.

Wright, Wendy M. *Bond of Perfection: Jeanne de Chantal and François de Sales.* New York: Paulist Press, 1985. Enhanced edition: Stella Niagara, NY: De Sales Resource Center, 2002.

——. *Francis de Sales: Introduction to the Devout Life and Treatise on the Love of God.* New York: Crossroad, 1993.

——. *A Retreat With Francis de Sales, Jane de Chantal and Aelred of Rievaulx: Befriending Each Other in God.* Cincinnati: St Anthony Messenger Press, 1996.

——. *Sacred Heart: Gateway to God.* Maryknoll, NY: Orbis, 2001. London: Darton, Longman and Todd, 2002.

Web Resources

Toward a Complete Bibliography of English Language Works. Compiled by Joseph Boenzi, SDB. http://www4.desales.edu/~salesian/fdsbibli.html

Collections of Salesian Resources

De Sales Resource Center
4421 Lower River Road
Stella Niagara, NY 14144
http://www.desalesresource.org

DeSales University
Trexler Library
2775 Station Avenue
Center Valley, PA 18034–9568 1

INDEX